To all those who row,
tirelessly and often unheralded,
for the purity of a common goal.

DOUG,
THANKS FOR THE OPPORTUNITY
TO HELP WITH YOUR HOUSE
SALE.
Kim + Stefana

The narrow race course through the Montlake Cut and under the historic Montlake Bridge is one of many unique features of the Windermere Cup regatta in Seattle.

Photo: Joel W. Rogers Photography

The
WINDERMERE CUP

*A history of one of
the world's premier rowing regattas*

WRITTEN BY GREGG BELL

The Windermere Cup: A history of one of the world's premier rowing regattas

Windermere Real Estate Services Company
5424 Sand Point Way NE, Seattle, WA 98105
(206) 527-3801
www.windermere.com

First Edition
Printed in South Korea

Author: Gregg Bell
General Manager: Shelley Rossi
Managing Editor: Christine M. Fairchild, Fairchild Press, Seattle, Washington
Proofreader: Sheryl Madden
Book Designer: Patricia Bradbury, PB Design & Branding
Publisher: Windermere Real Estate Services Company
Printing Management: StarPrint Brokers, Inc., Bellevue, Washington

ISBN: 978-0-578-17825-7
Library of Congress Cataloging in Publication Data
Sports and Recreation

TABLE OF CONTENTS

Cover photo: Scott Eklund/Red Box Pictures

Photo: Olivia Bedoyan, Photographer

Introduction

by John W. Jacobi

Founder, Windermere Real Estate

PEOPLE MIGHT be surprised to know that I'm not a rower. That is to say, I rowed a few times back when I was a young man in the US Coast Guard, but never competitively. And I never had aspirations to get involved with the sport of rowing.

But that all changed in May of 1986 when I read Blaine Newnham's column in the *Seattle Times* about the University of Washington's elite rowing program.

Actually, if memory serves me right, Newnham was criticizing the Huskies for not bringing better competition to one of the most idyllic rowing settings in the world for a race against one of the best rowing programs in the US. His rant led me to set up a meeting with then UW rowing director Dick Erickson and women's coach Bob Ernst to discuss an event that could bring world-class rowers to Seattle's Montlake Cut.

Rain or sun, fans line the Montlake Bridge, a bascule drawbridge in the Gothic-style designed by Carl F. Gould, one of the original architects for the University of Washington campus.

The rest is history and the basis for this book.

Over the past thirty years, rowing has become a part of the fabric of my life. Because of Windermere Cup, I have grandchildren who row competitively and our family is pretty passionate about this sport which very few of us knew much about before 1987. The deep relationship we've built with our partners, the University of Washington and the Seattle Yacht Club, is invaluable. With a list of logistics a mile long, we somehow come together each year and put on one of Seattle's largest community events. Even after thirty years, I'm still in awe.

There are a lot of ways to give back to a community and many causes out there to support—and we do both at Windermere Real Estate. But one of the things I'm most proud of is this event. It's a gift we're humbled to give to this community that has given so much to us. ∎

Foreword

by Blaine Newnham

Former *Seattle Times* columnist

I'M ENAMORED with sports stadiums, and have been since first walking into the home baseball park of the Oakland Oaks of the Pacific Coast League.

That was more than sixty years ago.

As a young baseball writer, I visited Crosley Field in Cincinnati, Forbes Field in Pittsburgh, and Connie Mack Stadium in Philadelphia, all the year before the old stadiums were replaced. I was lucky to be in old Yankee Stadium with the monuments in the outfield, in Boston Garden with the parquet floor. I wrote stories from Mac Court at the University of Oregon, the old and new Olympic Stadiums in Greece, and the heavenly golf settings—if not stadiums—of Augusta National and St. Andrews.

We have such a setting in Seattle, a true Carnegie Hall of Rowing: the Montlake Cut.

I love rowing, even though I've never rowed. As a student at Cal (University of California, Berkeley), I watched the Bears row on the Oakland Estuary, a couple of miles from where I was born. The rowers were so tall, so elegant, so confident.

Multi-colored oars line the pier of UW's Conibear Shellhouse.

After graduating, I worked for the university doing PR for Cal's rowing team, a year Cal won the Intercollegiate Rowing Association (IRA) National Championship. I reveled in our yearly dual match with Washington.

I'd heard about Opening Day in Seattle but didn't quite understand what it had to do with rowing. Then, when I was working at the *Seattle Times*, I saw the thousands of spectators lining the Cut, some up on the Gothic bridge that separates the campus from Capitol Hill, awaiting the parade of yachts to follow the crew races.

The Huskies are always an imposing crew, and I guess it was to be expected that they'd win every race that day in 1986, as if there was no competition. Well, there wasn't.

Oregon State had come north to be the sacrificial lambs. For my column the next day in the *Times*, instead of going on and on about the beauty of rowing and the synchronized strokes and paddles in the water, I took the Huskies to task.

Why waste the world's best setting for a race that is no race at all? Bring in a powerhouse like Harvard and find a sponsor to finance it.

> **"The first Windermere Cup was, for me, one of the great moments I've witnessed in sports."**
>
> BLAINE NEWNHAM

Instead of being perturbed, Dick Erickson, the great UW coach, called to thank me for the idea and the motivation. It's now history that John Jacobi read my column, called Erickson, and a year later made the Windermere Cup a reality.

I never imagined the Soviet Union would show up as the first invited guests, but I should have. I'd been in Moscow the year before for the Goodwill Games, the first meeting of US and Soviet athletes since the boycott of the 1980 Olympics in Moscow. Bob Walsh, the Seattle sports promoter, was bringing the second Goodwill Games to Seattle in 1990. He could get the world's greatest crew to Seattle if anyone could.

The first Windermere Cup was, for me, one of the great moments I've witnessed in sports. Not so much the slashing power of the Soviets in dominating the race, but the free exchange afterward as the rowers not only traded shirts, but split up and shared the two shells. One of the Huskies, wearing a Soviet shirt and rowing with four Soviets back to the shell house, said he'd never felt such thrust in a boat.

It was great theater befitting a great venue. So far from the Oakland Estuary, where tugs and barges and pleasure boats meander through an industrial channel while the crews try to race. The Cut was surely better than the rowing venue for the 1968 Olympic Games in Mexico City, where only the finish was visible for the few spectators on hand.

International rowing is like that. The 1984 Olympics were held on a reservoir outside Los Angeles. Bob Ernst coached

A women's eight crew competing in the 2012 Windermere Cup.

those US women to victory. It was exciting, but who really saw it?

It's too bad the IRA can't change its format and stage the championship race in the Cut. Have four lanes instead of eight, cutting the field with two semifinal races. That will never happen, but then, who thought the Windermere Cup would?

As the years passed, crews from everywhere came to Seattle. Some of the rowers came back to compete for the Huskies.

It is interesting that Washington's grand program, the pride of the school, is better now than it has ever been. For me, the news of their exploits gets needlessly lost in results of the women's softball team or the men's golf team. Rowing is special. Those who do it understand. Windermere understands.

With the new shell house by the lake, Washington's crew commands the best home in the sport, and with Windermere, the Huskies have the best invitational race in the sport. There is open water on the lake for year-round training, and then there's that funneling of water and boats through the Montlake Cut to Lake Union.

A warm, sunlit spring day makes any Opening Day a grand spectacle. Windermere has made Opening Day special no matter the wind or the wet. ∎

The Windermere Cup Makes International Sports History

ANDREJ VASILJEV couldn't believe his eyes. Or his ears. The rower for the Soviet Union's national eight-man crew was rowing amid roars of ten thousand-plus spectators lining the banks of the Montlake Cut on a cold, rainy morning in Seattle.

It was May 2, 1987. A USSR men's crew had never competed in Washington state, and now Vasiljev's team was winning one of the few non-Olympic athletic competitions for the Soviets inside the US in twenty-five years. Since the time of the 1962 Cuban Missile Crisis.

After sixteen years of hosting a regional regatta on the Opening Day of Seattle's boating season, and dominating visiting crews, UW was hosting its most competitive rowing spectacle yet.

Ten minutes earlier, at 11:25 a.m., the first women's Windermere Cup race began between the University of Washington, the University of California, and the Soviet Union.

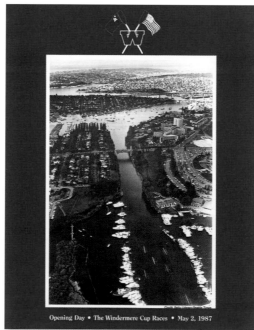

Opening Day • The Windermere Cup Races • May 2, 1987

A flyer announcing the first year of the Windermere Cup in 1987. Thereafter, a unique poster was created for each year's event.

A Soviet women's crew had never rowed in the US, let alone in Seattle.

The Huskies' women's crew started fast, but the older, more-experienced Soviets were steady in their strokes and speed and took the lead early in the 2,000-meter course that led out to Union Bay on the edge of Lake Washington, then sliced through the Montlake Cut, the narrow channel linking Lake Union to Lake Washington.

The USSR opened a boat-length lead over the first half of the course, starting from the long log boom that stretched toward Lake Washington and anchored a fleet of spectators' boats.

As the crews approached the Montlake Bridge, about 700 meters from the finish line, the Soviets' lead grew to almost two boat lengths.

Fans scrambled from the east edge of the bridge to the west side as the Soviets, and then the Huskies, rowed beneath them. Cal was far behind throughout.

Bells rang amid screams from spectators standing under rain ponchos, tarps, and umbrellas as the Soviets crossed the finish line three boat lengths ahead of the Huskies, whose six-race winning streak in the Opening Day Regatta ended. The Soviet women waved to the cheering crowd from their drifting boat following the win.

WINNING THEIR OWN BATTLE

Back at the start line, more than 2,000 meters to the east, Vasiljev and his Soviet crewmates readied to begin the first Windermere Cup men's race. They and the Huskies were the only two crews in the field.

The Soviet men's national eight-man crew raced in the inaugural Windermere Cup, 1987.

They shot off in a steady rain at 11:35.

The Soviets were from Leningrad and Vilnius and Kiev and Kherson, all in their mid-twenties or older. Many were in the Soviet Army. The Soviets' coxswain, Grigory Dmi-trienko, was forty-two years old. He'd won a bronze medal in the eight-man Olympic final at the 1980 Moscow Games. In an unorthodox arrangement for this first Windermere Cup, he was forward in the Soviets' borrowed, West German-made shell rather than aft.

Vasiljev and his comrades were even more dominant through the Montlake Cut than the Soviet women had been.

Eight powerboats trailed the two crews as they sliced

across Union Bay toward the Montlake Bridge.

The Soviet Union's lead was nearly two boat lengths.

With the crowd roaring from the grassy banks along Montlake Cut, with horns blaring from boats moored near the finish line, the Soviets won that first Windermere Cup by almost four boat lengths and fifteen seconds.

"I never heard a single word of the coxswain during the race, the people were so loud," Vasiljev said later that day.

"Even the finals of the world championships are not as impressive as this."

CALLING A HISTORIC RACE

That first Saturday in May 1987 had dawned wet and cold in Seattle. The Soviet men's and women's rowing teams ate breakfast at Haggett Hall and then, back at the dormitory, changed into their iconic red racing uniforms with the familiar gold hammer-and-sickle logos. They brought a change of clothes to don immediately after the race during their van ride back to the Huskies' crew house. By 10 a.m. they were in yet another secure area for prerace instructions.

Forty-five minutes later, the women's crews launched from the shell house and rowed their way the mile or so across

---

DICK ERICKSON

The Coach with the Red Pickup Truck

Dick Erickson—and his trusty red truck—were as Husky as the UW.

The native of Arlington, Washington, headed straight to the University of Washington out of Arlington High School in 1954. By the time he left the Huskies' rowing program, he had competed against the Soviets and at Henley. He was a member of UW's varsity eight boat that traveled to England for the 1958 Henley Royal Regatta, where the Huskies fell to the Leningrad Trud Rowing Club.

Erickson and those Huskies, coached by Husky Hall-of-Fame-member Al Ulbrickson, then challenged the Leningrad boat to a rematch. The Washington crew avenged their loss at Henley by beating the Soviets in Moscow. That race, broadcast by legendary ABC Sports broadcaster Keith Jackson, then of Seattle's KOMO Radio, is believed to be the first sporting event aired to the West from behind the Soviet Union's Iron Curtain.

His standout performance on that 1958 Husky team got Erickson elected to the Husky Hall of Fame in 1984. He graduated in

UW's Class of '58 with a bachelor's degree in physical education. In 1964 he received a master's degree in education administration from Harvard.

That was also his first year coaching the Huskies' freshman crew team. Four years later, in 1968, he took over UW's powerhouse men's varsity program—and stayed for the next twenty-nine years.

In his first twenty years, Erickson led the Huskies to fifteen Pacific Coast rowing championships, the Intercollegiate Rowing Association National Championship in 1970 (though from 1982-96 the race was known as the National Collegiate Rowing Championship), and the title at the 1984 national university championship regatta in

Cincinnati. In 1977, his crew won the Grand Challenge Cup at Henley. That Husky crew went on to compete at the Nile Invitational Regatta in Cairo, Egypt.

But Erickson was a Husky far beyond the water. He was renowned for helping any and every UW student-athlete, fellow coach, staffer or teacher in any capacity. Before one memorable, chilled Apple Cup football game in the 1970s, Erickson thawed frozen pipes at Husky Stadium. Invariably, on campus and off, Erickson would pull up in his ever-present red pickup truck and offer to help.

He was the Pac-10 rowing coach of the year three times, and he was a member of the US Olympic Rowing Committee from 1972-75. He retired from coaching following the 1987 season, then became the facilities manager for the UW Department of Intercollegiate Athletics, where he was in charge of day-to-day operations for various Husky athletic facilities.

He died at the age of sixty-five in July of 2001. He was survived by his wife, Irma, and their sons Alan, Jeff, and Jon. ∎

Union Bay, around the newly extended log boom at the starting line, and into open water beyond Montlake Cut. The men's crews followed close behind.

While thousands of spectators surrounded the Cut to see this international showdown on the water, a regional television audience tuned into Seattle's KOMO for "Opening Day '87, the US versus the USSR."

"Windermere Cup" had yet to catch on as the event's title.

Fittingly, Keith Jackson was co-anchoring KOMO's telecast with Bruce King, the station's veteran sports director. Jackson, the legendary voice of ABC Sports, had already been part of a seminal moment in the history of Husky crew and UW athletics.

In 1958, the State Department had approved arrangements for Washington's varsity eight to row in Moscow as

> 66 Even the finals of the world championships are not as impressive as this. 99
>
> ANDREJ VASILJEV

UW's men's crew hosted the USSR, its toughest competition yet in an Opening Day race.

the first US team to compete behind the Iron Curtain.

On their way to that race in the USSR, the Huskies met the Soviets' Leningrad Trud Rowing Club at England's famed Royal Henley Regatta. Leningrad Trud beat UW by one and one-half boat lengths over a one-mile, 550-yard course to win the Grand Challenge Cup on the River Thames.

They held the rematch fifteen days later in Moscow.

Washington stunned the older Leningrad Trud and three Soviet crews on the 2,000-meter Khimkinskow Reservoir course to win the Moscow Cup by one and three-quarter lengths.

Jackson called that historic race, one of the greatest upsets in rowing history, back to the US on Seattle's KOMO Radio, which was believed to be the first sports broadcast by a Western outlet from behind the Iron Curtain.

Rowers get an inspiring view from under the Montlake Bridge of both its classic architecture and the roaring fans.

Photo: Scott Eklund/Red Box Pictures

For the 1987 Windermere Cup, Jackson began his waterside broadcast with this: "Nice to be part of a little piece of history. I'm glad to see the weather hasn't changed, and neither has the indefatigable spirit of the web-footed locals."

What to this day makes the Windermere Cup course and its setting so unique is the proximity of racers to the screaming fans crowding the sloped banks on both sides of the Cut. If crews row side by side through the channel, spectators can be within a dozen feet of the action. Essentially, this one-of-a-kind course is like crew racing inside a stadium.

"They were so good," Blaine Newnham, then a columnist with the *Seattle Times*, said twenty-five years later of those Soviets at the first Windermere Cup.

Former UW director of rowing Bob Ernst, then three years removed from winning Olympic gold, wasn't used to a crew of his getting handled so easily. Yet he wasn't exactly irate that day, either. "I mean, I had seen them for years at the world championships and at the Olympics," Ernst said. "And they were the real deal."

BUILDING GOODWILL

More than fifty years after the *The Boys in the Boat* crew made Washington rowing world-famous, the Windermere Cup race result was secondary. Something more lasting was about to occur.

Minutes after the Soviets and Huskies men crossed the finish line to conclude the first regatta held by Windermere Real Estate, UW's boat and the Soviets' shell idled side by side. Competitors turned comrades, the rowers began switching racing jerseys.

Four Soviets carefully stood in their boat. While the Huskies held

> " **I mean, I had seen them for years at the world championships and at the Olympics…And they were the real deal.** "
>
> BOB ERNST

The USSR rowers lift a celebratory drink as they mingle aboard Frank Dupar Jr.'s yacht on their way to a dinner party at John W. Jacobi's house.

the edges of their borrowed West German shell, the Soviets took slow, measured steps across and into UW's boat.

Then four Huskies clambered over the sidewall of the Soviet's boat, so each boat contained four Soviets in UW's white and purple jerseys and four Huskies in the Soviets' red jerseys.

That's how these supposed political arch-enemies, Americans and Soviets, completed a celebratory, cooperative, unforgettable row back to the boathouse. Supposed foes, united by sport.

This was a world-news-making moment far from the cameras of still-neophyte CNN. It was four years before the Berlin Wall crashed down, the time of US President Ronald Reagan's and USSR Communist Party General Secretary Mikhail Gorbachev's *glasnost*—years before most Americans had even heard of the word.

"That was the greatest thing that happened that whole week," Lois Kipper, hostess to dozens of visiting crews for the first decade-plus of Windermere Cups, said of the post-race jersey swap. "I'm sure their security and coaches were in a state of apoplexy. But our athletes loved it. Their athletes loved it. It was such a great scene."

For about twenty minutes the two crews rowed back through the Montlake Cut, across Union Bay to the docks of the UW's Conibear Shellhouse, marking Seattle's new Opening Day Regatta as an international milestone.

More than a quarter century later, that signature moment, not the result of the race, is how the first Windermere Cup is remembered.

"It was the damndest thing," said Newnham, a champion of UW's rowing cause. "It was a wonderful Evil

Empire moment."

That scene was the inspiration behind the 2011 Windermere Cup poster, the twenty-fifth anniversary of the race, and set the tone of brotherhood, colorful personalities, and international goodwill that has marked the Windermere Cup's history.

But that wasn't the only goodwill moment that first regatta. Frank Dupar Jr.'s yacht, *Tranquility Base*, hosted the Soviets for the cruise to the house of Windermere Real Estate owner John Jacobi for the party the night before. Because of its mammoth size and the owner's friendship with Jacobi, *Tranquility Base* was also a VIP boat for the first Cup races. She carried friends and supporters of Windermere and the UW to the regatta and the annual boat parade immediately following the race.

After the crew race, many Soviet and Husky rowers also

The USSR's men's crew on the dock behind UW's Conibear Shellhouse after winning the first Windermere Cup on May 2, 1987.

boarded the craft to watch the boat parade.

As *Tranquility Base* was about to dock so the crews could go ashore for a Saturday night out, Jacobi was waving goodbye to the VIPs.

One of the members of the Soviet contingent ran up to the Windermere chief, frantic.

In broken English, yet in the sternest, most urgent tone any Soviet had used all week, the official informed Jacobi that a member of the USSR's men's team was missing.

Coaches and police and KGB agents scrambled, talking urgently on walkie-talkies and searching every corner of Dupar's eighty-foot boat, plus the water and docks and land around it.

Well, they didn't search the yacht's *every* corner.

Amid the panic, Dupar approached Jacobi on the sly, away from Soviet officials' ears. Amused but somewhat puzzled,

Dupar told his friend he'd found the Soviet guy, plus the second missing rower. A UW woman rower.

They were, ahem, intertwined inside the engine room.

"I don't know how to get them out of there," Dupar said. "They're passed out."

"Well," Jacobi said, "start the engine!"

Dupar did, and the newly formed comrades nearly completed another international athletic feat.

"God, they jumped up," the Windermere chief said later with a big laugh. "There you go. There's your first ..."

Ernst also chuckled at the incident. "Outreach program," he called it.

HOSTING, AMERICAN STYLE

Race day wasn't the end of the Soviets' stay in Seattle in 1987.

The Sunday after the Soviets' victory started with breakfast inside UW's Haggett Hall dormitory, their home for that historic week. Then the contingent of two dozen Soviets rode downtown to the studios of KING television, the local NBC affiliate, where they spent three hours recording a special program detailing their race and their week of events that preceded it.

The Soviets then joined the Huskies and both teams' coaches cruising Seattle's Elliott Bay, and eventually landing at Tillicum Village on Blake Island, eight miles across the water from downtown Seattle. The rowers and coaches learned about Northwest Native American cultures and enjoyed a salmon-buffet lunch next to Blake Island State Park. The Soviets were, for an afternoon, Pacific Northwesterners.

"I thought it was nice we got to show them our native culture," said Kipper. "It was a little touristy, but the Soviets had a good time. And it was good they had freedom to explore around on the boat getting there and back."

After the Tillicum Village tour, they sauntered around downtown Seattle, with their coaches in tow, whom Ernst

April Kieburtz, retired Windermere franchise owner, posing with the Soviet rowers on a yacht cruise.

had suspected all week of being KGB agents. At 10 p.m. the rowers finally got back from their most packed day of their stay.

Monday morning the Soviets went out on the water again. The women rowed with the Huskies' women's team in mixed boats, then went to UW's weight room to test their strength. The visitors then went on a four-hour tour of Lake Washington via UW's Waterfront Activities Center.

By afternoon, back on land, the Communist visitors were enthralled by vendors throwing fish behind counters in one of Seattle's iconic halls of capitalism: Pike Place Market. They even posed for pictures sitting on Rachel the Pig, the market's bronze, street-side mascot and giant piggy bank.

Their final night the Soviets were hosted at a goodbye dinner in the Conibear Shellhouse with the Huskies' crew teams and coaches.

More than a quarter century after she helped usher the Soviets around Seattle, Kipper remains amazed by how accommodating Windermere was for the rowers. "I just keep thinking how generous Windermere was for these athletes, and how earnestly the company tried to accommodate their every need. How Windermere went to great lengths to integrate them with the other host athletes (from UW)," Kipper said. "We six hostesses were just there to pick up the slack and help out where we were needed."

After the farewell dinner, Washington men's rowing coach Dick Erickson pulled his trusty red pickup truck, the one that had shuttled Team USSR's gear for the last week, back up to Haggett Hall. He loaded the bags of the athletes who had humbled his Huskies on the water. Erickson then drove his truck behind the Soviets' buses to SeaTac Airport, where at 12:30 a.m. the Soviets boarded Northwest Flight 50 for a red-eye to Minneapolis, an early morning connection to Washington-National, a transfer by bus to Dulles Airport, then the long Aeroflot flight back to Moscow.

Windermere and Washington had succeeded in turning

Seattle's local boating-day celebration into an international showcase with, remarkable for the time, no defections.

That showcase would go on to attract crews from China, Egypt, Australia, England, South Africa, Great Britain, Poland, Germany, the Czech Republic, Belarus, and Croatia, among others. Word spread in the global rowing community about the jewel Windermere and UW had created.

The Cup would soon enrich countless lives and change many others across the globe. ■

BOB ERNST

From Playing the Rose Bowl to Entering Rowing's Hall of Fame

Southern California native Bob Ernst brought a unique athletic background to Husky crew.

After graduating from Costa Mesa High School in 1963, he played center for the Orange Coast College football team that played in the "Junior Rose Bowl," the national junior-college championship game. Ernst's OCC team beat Northeastern Oklahoma A&M 21-0 in front of 44,044 fans at the Rose Bowl in Pasadena. That game was played two and a half weeks after the assassination of John F. Kennedy.

Ernst also was on the swimming and water polo teams at Orange Coast College, then enrolled at UC Irvine and continued on its swimming and water-polo teams. Ernst joined Irvine's rowing program in 1966 and, as a senior in 1967, he was its team captain. He graduated that year and was inducted into UC-Irvine athletics' Hall of Fame in 1984.

Ernst was seven years out of college and coaching rowing at his alma mater when he brought his UC-Irvine crew to the North-west in spring 1974, and his unknown Ant-eaters nearly upset Dick Erickson's heavily favored Huskies.

Husky legend Erickson was so impressed he offered Ernst a job as UW's freshman coach. Ernst jumped at the chance to leave his native Orange County and join a national powerhouse program.

In 1979, while in his fifth year as UW's freshman coach, Ernst earned a master's degree in sports administration from Washington. He took over the men's program and director of rowing from Erickson in 1987.

Over the next twenty years Ernst's teams won two national championships (in 1997 and 2007), eleven conference titles, eleven Pacific-10 Conference coach-of-the-year awards, and fifteen Windermere Cup finals.

During that time he also coached fourteen Olympians. He began coaching the United States national team in 1976 and stayed until 1988, leading four Olympic teams. In 1984, at the Los Angeles Games, Ernst led the US women's eight-oared boat to gold.

It was his international rowing excellence that got him inducted into the sport's national Hall of Fame in 1994.

After that 2007 national title, Ernst turned the men's program over to one of his former Husky rowers, Michael Callahan, and became women's coach again. In all, Ernst won eight national championships at Washington.

He continued as the women's crew coach and was the key coordinator who secured international crews for each year's Windermere Cup until his departure in November of 2015. ■

An eight-man crew racing its shell in the Windermere Cup regatta. This is the view fans get when watching the race from the Montlake Bridge.

Bringing the Soviets during the Cold War

S EATTLE, the entire West Coast, plus rowers and rowing enthusiasts from Massachusetts to Moscow, can thank John Jacobi for reading the Sunday paper.

Jacobi is the aggressive, gregarious former owner and CEO of Windermere Real Estate, a franchise company based in Seattle. Jacobi purchased the company in 1972, and by 2016 Windermere Real Estate included about 300 offices operated by 110 franchisees across eleven states and Mexico. By 2015, Windermere was the largest regional real estate company in the Western US.

The genesis for the Windermere Cup Regatta came on a sunny Sunday morning in mid-May, 1986. Jacobi was on the back patio of his Seattle home he and his wife, Roz, shared near the Windermere home office, thumbing through his copy of the *Seattle Times* to the sports section. His eyes came upon the regular sports column written by Blaine Newnham, long an advocate for University of Washington athletics, and Husky

WINDERMERE CUP RACES

May 4 ~ Montlake Cut ~ 10:20 a.m.   Beijing ~ Great Britain ~ Stanford ~ Washington

Windermere

2002 poster

rowing in particular.

Newnham had written about Opening Day, the beginning of Seattle's boating season and the corresponding rowing regatta Washington had hosted the previous day on the Montlake Cut, the waterway bordering UW campus between Union and Portage bays.

"In front of an enormous Opening-Day Regatta crowd at the Montlake Cut, the Huskies beat up on Oregon State," Newnham wrote. "They squandered the moment, boring tens of thousands of spectators. They simply couldn't attract top-flight competition."

To Jacobi, this was a call to action.

"I thought, 'I've got to find some way to get connected with the university,'" Jacobi said of his company. "Football wasn't the way. I love football and I love basketball, but those programs already had a plethora of corporate sponsors. Unlike rowing."

Reading about UW's snooze of a crewrace that anchored

Opening Day hit him like an oar broken free from its lock.

"This just came out of the blue with this article," he said. "I thought, 'My gosh! This is so natural for us. And it would be so much fun.'"

FINDING THE PERFECT FIT

Seattle and rowing is a natural fit—has been since before 1911, in fact.

That's when Hiram Conibear, then Washington's rowing coach (and now the man whose name is on the Huskies' impressive boathouse Windermere helped fund) got Englishmen George and Dick Pocock to come build crew shells at UW. The Pocock Rowing Center, across the University Bridge from UW where Portage Bay meets Lake Union, became renowned as the premier masters- and junior-rowing facility in the Pacific Northwest.

And Jacobi, a Northwest native, had some experience on the water, though not in ul-tra-competitive rowing.

"No, actually I did row. I was in the Coast Guard and I rowed an eight-man whaleboat," he said. "I was the stroke and almost died. Ever row a whaleboat? Jesus. Weighs about four tons."

Jacobi explained his father, Lee, played football at Washington, though "he wasn't very successful." Indeed, on UW football's all-time rosters, there are no records of a Jacobi earning a varsity letter in football. "But I wanted to be a part of the university. Our company is very involved in the university, always has been," John Jacobi said. "We have a lot of friends and members of Windermere that are in various positions there."

The day after Jacobi read Newnham's column, the real estate chief traveled a mere five minutes from his Windermere office down Seattle's Sand Point Way to the University of Washington campus.

There he met with Dick Erickson, the iconic, tireless, drill-sergeant-like director of rowing for the Huskies. In 1970 Erickson and his Washington crew were invited by the Seattle Yacht Club to create a regatta as a "warm up" to the SYC's annual Opening Day boat parade. The Huskies proceeded to win twelve of the first sixteen opening regattas against local and regional competition. In that time they also won two national championships. It was Erickson who opened the sport to women at UW in 1975.

Jacobi's meeting with Erickson that day also included Bob

JOHN W. JACOBI

Invested in Home Teams for More than Half a Century

John Jacobi's home teams have been the same for half a century: the University of Washington and Windermere Real Estate.

Jacobi's father, Lee, was a former Washington Huskies football player, public-relations director of the Seattle Chamber of Commerce, and advertising chief executive in Seattle.

John Jacobi followed dad by graduating from the University of Washington in 1962. Soon after he began working for Puget Sound Mutual Savings Bank. He stayed there ten years, rising to the chief of the bank's residential real estate mortgage department. By then he realized he wanted to own his own company, and by the 1970s he'd acquired the business acumen and knowledge of Seattle's housing market to start one in real estate.

In 1972 he struck out on his own by purchasing an eight-person real estate company called Windermere Realty just off Sand Point Way, a couple miles north of the UW campus.

More than forty years later, the headquarters of Windermere Real Estate, the West's largest regional real estate company, was still on Sand Point Way in Seattle's Laurelhurst neighborhood.

"In the early years of Windermere, we knew we wanted to be different from other real estate companies," Jacobi wrote on the eve of his company's fortieth anniversary in 2012. "While others were focused on being number one in size or sales, we aspired to be the most respected."

Jacobi still feels one of his greatest honors was winning an independent survey ranking the most respected company brands in Washington State by Puget Sound Business Journal in 2011. Windermere competed with the likes of Microsoft Corporation, the University of Washington, Nordstrom, and Starbucks. Windermere got 58.8 percent of the votes for most respected brand in the real estate category. The next competitor got 16 percent.

"Our goal was to turn the traditional real estate model on its head by focusing first on community, because only then can you truly understand and anticipate the needs of those who live within the communities," Jacobi said. "Over the years, our owners and agents have embraced this approach with zeal through the Windermere Foundation, our annual Community Service Day, and their own local involvement and projects."

Such as the Windermere Cup. Jacobi and

Ernst, the affable, energetic women's crew coach at Washington at the time. "He said, 'Oh, my God! You've got this great event. You've got this great venue. And you are racing Oregon State,'" recalls Ernst, a born talker, recruiter, and rowing advocate who eventually took over for Erickson and led Husky crew until 2015.

Erickson knew he and his athletic director at Washington, Mike Lude, needed another group on board with Jacobi's idea to bolster the Opening Day Regatta.

"Bob, Dick and I met with Frank Young of the Seattle Yacht Club," Lude said. "They were really interested in making Opening Day of the boating season bigger, too.

"Let me tell you something: I don't know squat about rowing," said Lude, a former United States Marine Corps officer, assistant college football coach and college head baseball coach at Hillsdale and Maine. "But it didn't take me two weeks to see that rowing was a traditional and very big part of Husky athletics. My thought was to help rowing."

UW created the rowing regatta in 1987 at the prompting of a Seattle newspaper column a year earlier that challenged the Huskies to schedule tougher opponents for the annual Opening Day of the Northwest's boating season.

Challenge met. For the first race, Jacobi replaced Oregon State with the Soviet Union.

The Windermere Cup has thrived with international powers delighting tens of thousands in the Seattle community each first Saturday in May ever since.

Jacobi's personal touches to the Cup have included hosting the first prerace party at his northeast Seattle waterfront home. "We decided we'd have dinner for the athletes at our place the night before the event," Jacobi said. "But that was the last time we did it at our house."

The Soviets and a howling storm in May 1987 nearly ruined the Jacobi family's white carpeting. "After a while my wife, Roz, and I just looked at the house and it was trashed." Jacobi said.

The Communist rowers spent much of that memorable night with Jacobi's teenaged children conducting an international swap meet.

"All of our kids had jeans," Jacobi said. "And jeans were a big deal to the Soviets. They were trying them on. Or our kids would give the Soviets cassette tapes or trade for sweatshirts or whatever paraphernalia the Soviets had."

The Windermere Cup grew from there much like his company: extraordinarily.

"Windermere has always focused on three

JOHN W. JACOBI

basic principles: hire the best people; give them the best tools; create thriving communities," Jacobi said. "It's not rocket science, but it has worked pretty well for us for more than four decades."

Smashingly well. In those forty-plus years Jacobi's one-office, eight-person company grew to 300 offices and 8,000 agents.

In 2014 the elder Jacobi officially passed the company on to his son-in-law Geoff Wood,

daughter Jill Jacobi Wood, and son OB Jacobi.

And the Seattle real estate patriarch sat proudly watching his home teams: Windermere and the Huskies, just as he had for more than forty years. "My dad played football at the university, and I wanted to remain a part of the university," Jacobi said. ■

With that, what had for sixteen years been regional crew races coinciding with Seattle's Opening Day boat parade became the Windermere Cup, a world-renowned spectacle along a unique, man-made cut of water south of Washington's Husky Stadium.

"I had no idea it would grow into this. I didn't even know we'd be allowed to call it the Windermere Cup," Jacobi said. "I thought, they will probably want to name it after some famous rower or something. So that was a big deal."

So was the real estate man's ambitions for his new event.

INVITING THE RUSSIANS

When Jacobi met with Ernst and Erickson that Monday in May of 1986, he asked the coaches, "Who's the best team in the world?"

They informed Jacobi that the Soviets had won the World Rowing Championship in the women's eight and took second in the men's eight that year.

"Can we get those guys?" Jacobi asked.

"Well, we can try," Ernst replied. "And in 1987, they were there."

Of course, it was far from that easy.

"Remember," Jacobi explains, "this was the Cold War."

Five years before the Berlin Wall was to fall, to be exact. President Reagan was trying to get the US Congress to approve his so-called "Star Wars" policy, his Strategic Defense Initiative for the United States to have a space-based defense program against the threat of ballistic missiles from the Soviet Union.

USSR's leader, Mikhail Gorbachev, was a year into his tenure as the general secretary of the Soviet Communist party. May 1986 was still five months before Reagan and Gorbachev would meet in Reykjavik, Iceland, for a thawing summit that would begin turning the American president away from his hardline stance against the USSR.

The Soviets and fourteen of its Communist-bloc allies

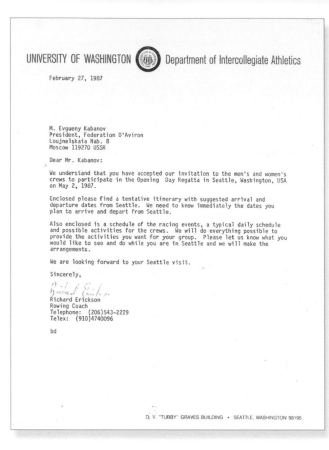

UNIVERSITY OF WASHINGTON — Department of Intercollegiate Athletics

February 27, 1987

M. Evgueny Kabanov
President, Federation D'Aviron
Loujnelskaia Nab. 8
Moscow 119270 USSR

Dear Mr. Kabanov:

We understand that you have accepted our invitation to the men's and women's crews to participate in the Opening Day Regatta in Seattle, Washington, USA on May 2, 1987.

Enclosed please find a tentative itinerary with suggested arrival and departure dates from Seattle. We need to know immediately the dates you plan to arrive and depart from Seattle.

Also enclosed is a schedule of the racing events, a typical daily schedule and possible activities for the crews. We will do everything possible to provide the activities you want for your group. Please let us know what you would like to see and do while you are in Seattle and we will make the arrangements.

We are looking forward to your Seattle visit.

Sincerely,

Richard Erickson
Rowing Coach
Telephone: (206)543-2229
Telex: (910)4740096

bd

D. V. "TUBBY" GRAVES BUILDING • SEATTLE, WASHINGTON 98195

UW rowing coach Dick Erickson telexed this letter to the USSR rowing federation confirming the Soviets' participation in the first Windermere Cup.

had boycotted the 1984 Olympic Games in Los Angeles. Most believed the Soviet boycott was in retaliation for the Americans and their allies boycotting the 1980 Games in Moscow, part of the Western world's protest to the Soviet invasion of Afghanistan at the end of the 1970s.

So American-Soviet relations hadn't exactly warmed yet when Ernst and Jacobi began the process of getting the USSR's national crew teams to Seattle for what would become the first Windermere Cup in 1987. "In 1986 it was still nitty-gritty, the Evil Empire versus Ronald Reagan, all that," Newnham said.

Newnham's column was the impetus; Jacobi's interest was the spark; and the UW team of Ernst and Erickson became the engine.

"Bob Ernst and Dick Erickson were so well connected internationally in rowing. They knew everybody, all over the world," Lude said. "And they were at such a high level organizationally and competitively. They energized the entire effort."

Erickson was "the consummate Husky," said Ernst, who went from leading the UW women's rowing program to taking charge of the men when Erickson retired in 1987. "He loved the University of Washington. He probably would have worked for free just because he loved the place."

Lude seconded Ernst. "Dick Erickson was the most loyal team player you could imagine," said Lude, an assistant football coach at Hillsdale College, the University of Maine, and the University of Delaware. He was also the head baseball coach at Hillsdale in 1948-49 and at Maine in '50-51.

How loyal was Erickson? Lude recalls the morning of the 1985 football Apple Cup, when UW hosted its archrival Washington State at Husky Stadium. It had been snowing in Seattle for five days, piling up to about a foot of accumulation and essentially shutting down the hilly city unaccustomed to such weather. Erickson showed up at the stadium at 5 a.m. on game day with shovels in his pickup truck and a pack of his rowers in tow.

Source: University of Washington

"Hey, boss," Erickson said to his AD, "where do I get to work?"

The coach and his rowers then helped clear the field and stands. They even helped keep the restrooms' pipes from freezing.

"Dick Erickson was just like a platoon sergeant," Lude said. "He knew how to get things done."

Including bringing the Soviets—and Ernst—to UW.

ENLISTING THE TROOPS

After almost losing to Ernst's UC Irvine crew in 1974, an impressed Erickson made Ernst Washington's freshman coach. In 1980 Erickson promoted him to become the UW's women's varsity coach. A year later, Washington's women won their first national overall team championship when Ernst's junior-varsity and varsity crews won NCAA titles.

Ernst's UW women's teams won six national championships. The sixth was in the season that included the 1987 Opening Day Regatta—and all the coordination it took to get the Soviets there for it.

After Erickson and Ernst had met with Jacobi and hatched the idea to ratchet up the competition of the Opening Day Regatta, to bring in the world's best and America's ideological opposite, Erickson went to his sports information director (SID) for UW rowing.

"Dick said, 'Hey, there's a man by the name of John Jacobi. He owns Windermere Real Estate, and he wants to help with the Opening Day crew races,'" Jeanne (Grainger) Hasenmiller, that assistant

> **" I don't know squat about rowing. But it didn't take me two weeks to see that rowing was a traditional and very big part of Husky athletics. "**
>
> MIKE LUDE

sports-information director, remembered.

The SID's response to her coach? "Okay, I'll put an ad in the program for Windermere."

"No," Erickson responded. "He doesn't want to just buy an ad; he wants to buy the whole event."

That sent Hasenmiller, Lude, Erickson, and Ernst off to meet with Frank Young, head of the SYC at that time. They knew the lifeblood of the boating season's Opening Day races was the close partnership UW rowing had built with the SYC. The club had established the Opening Day celebration decades before Husky crew joined, with races in 1970.

"It was their event and their schedule," Hasenmiller said.

Young and his club canvassed members for volunteers to provide everything from race-day setup to hosts and hostesses for the visiting Soviets for the entire week of the race. The SYC, Tyee Yacht Club in Seattle, Meydenbauer Bay Yacht Club across Lake Washington in Bellevue, and Vancouver, British Columbia, Yacht Club were among those in the

region that were starting masters' rowing programs to compete in Seattle's Opening Day Regatta.

Erickson had taught those teams—which included his wife Irma—the finer points of rowing. The women on first masters' teams, most in their forties, became known as "Dick's Chicks," many of whom became volunteer hostesses for the visiting teams of the Windermere Cup.

"When he and Jacobi came up with the idea for an international Windermere Cup and were finaliz-

Three generations of Jacobi men: (from right to left) John W. Jacobi, his son OB Jacobi, and OB's son, Dylan.

ing plans, they realized they needed some hosting to make it a big-time event. So we had to do it," said Lois Kipper, one of those "Dick's Chicks" who also competed in the masters' preliminary races of Cups through 2011. "And I gave good parties," Kipper joked. "That was right down my alley."

Catherine "Kit" Green, the Huskies' associate director of athletics in the 1980s, led the coordination effort for the athletic department. While she and Hasenmiller began planning the logistics of expanding boating's Opening Day with Kipper and her SYC members, the coaches had to get their athletic director's approval.

Any worries that the project would end at the athletic director's desk before it ever got off campus disappeared seconds after Lude heard the plan for the Huskies to challenge the Soviets.

"Let's go after that," Lude told Erickson and Ernst. "Hey, it's a heck of an idea."

Lude had a precedent in pulling off new, big events for Washington. About a half-dozen years earlier, he had collaborated in 1984 with Hartly Kruger, executive vice president of the Seattle-King County Convention and Visitors Bureau, to bring the NCAA men's basketball Final Four to the county-owned Kingdome for the first time. The concrete-domed stadium south of downtown Seattle hosted the Final Four again in 1989.

In between, Lude tapped into Kruger's political connections in Washington State and beyond to help him bring the Soviets to UW for the 1987 inaugural Windermere Cup.

Norm Dicks, US Congressman from Washington's 6th District (1977 to 2013), helped make inroads at the nation's capital. Dicks then attended the first Cup.

Lude also contacted Bob Walsh. By 1985, Walsh was coordinating with international sports administrators to bring to Seattle what became the 1990 Goodwill Games between athletes from the United States, the Soviet Union, and their allies.

Jacobi aligned with the Seattle entrepreneur and public-relations specialist, whose title then was President of the Goodwill Games Organizing Committee, knowing Walsh had ties to the US State Department and the Kremlin. Those connections, built in part through humanitarian efforts, helped cut through the bureaucratic red tape that could have

Even in the rain spectators line the banks of the Montlake Cut, where they can watch rowers fly past within twenty feet of reach.

Photo: Windermere Real Estate Services Company

doomed the first Windermere Cup inside someone's file folder.

"The Soviets had turned down the request to participate, and I talked with the Kremlin and Minister of Sport Marat Gramov," Walsh said, explaining that Gramov was the Soviet official who made the decision for the USSR not to participate in the 1984 Los Angeles Olympics, "not because of retaliation, as the world believes, but because the Soviets did not have a competitive team and used the boycott as an excuse."

"After my meetings with Moscow, they reversed their decision and felt the rowing event would be a good lead-in to the Goodwill Games," Walsh added.

Between Kruger's local connections, Dick's national ones, and Walsh's international ties, they got the US State Department involved in meeting with Lude, Ernst, and Erickson on the UW campus. Lude remembers those negotiations on how the Soviets' stay in Seattle would go as cordial and relatively snag-free. "It was no big deal," Lude said. "We weren't going to war. And we at UW had always had good contacts in Washington [D.C.]"

Those connections helped get the White House and the State Department on board with what was one of the first non-Olympics-related athletic competition for the Soviets in the United States in twenty-five years, since around the time of the 1962 Cuban Missile Crisis. Furthermore, a Soviet women's crew had never rowed in the United States. A USSR men's crew had never competed in Seattle.

GETTING THE SOVIETS TO COMMIT

Once Erickson, Ernst, Green, Hasenmiller, and Windermere's staff got Walsh involved and the idea floated, there was the not-so-small matter of getting the Soviets to commit to coming.

In 1987 it wasn't like Ernst could send an e-mail or a direct message through Twitter to the Soviet rowing federation asking for confirmation. There were embassies to go through, language barriers and time zones to navigate, telexes to write and wire across the Atlantic Ocean.

Green wrote a University of Washington "interdepartmental correspondence" to Lude dated November 24, 1986, over five months before the race, declaring: "If we don't have

Bob Walsh, the promoter who helped secure the Soviets for the inaugural Windermere Cup, sitting next to Lynne Cox, the American long-distance open-water swimmer who set world records crossing the English Channel and dared swim from Little Diomede Island in Alaska to Big Diomede, then part of the Soviet Union.

definite confirmation by mid-December, we cannot put this project together."

Another correspondence Green wrote on December 18, 1986 said, "As soon as Dick [Erickson] gets a positive response from the Russian contact, we should move ahead with planning."

And on February 27, 1987, Green ended a letter to Walsh asking for the Soviets' tentative travel itinerary with this: "We also need written confirmation by letter or telex that the Russians intend to participate in the event."

Later that same day, only nine weeks before race day, Erickson acknowledged to Evgueny Kabanov, then president of Federation D'Aviron, the Soviet Union's rowing federation: "We understand that you have accepted our invitation for men's and women's crews to participate in the Opening-Day Regatta in Seattle, Washington, USA, on May 2, 1987... We need to know immediately the dates you plan to arrive and depart from Seattle."

"It was just a miracle," Jacobi said of finally getting an official "da" out of Moscow. "Then it was, 'Okay, what does that mean?'"

First, it meant knowing what to call the visitors.

"We were straightened out early on: 'You can't call these people Russians,'" Ernst explained. "They aren't just Russians. Most of the women were Lithuanians, and they didn't like the Russians at all. They were on the national team because it was a big deal, but they didn't want to be called Russians or be associated with the Russians, even though they were all part of the Soviet Union."

A Soviet yes also meant coordination with campus, city, state, regional, and federal agencies. It meant details on everything from rental vans to accommodations to the new race trophy to banquets, even to which logo to put on the hundred commemorative sweaters the UW wanted to present to the Soviet athletes (eventually they decided on Windermere's company logo).

"That was just huge," Ernst said, laughing about all the coordination that went into the first Windermere Cup. "That's so interesting."

Security was the first and last concern, and fortunately Husky crew had a friend atop the Seattle Police Department. Patrick Fitzsimons was Seattle's police chief from 1979-94.

BOB WALSH

The Citizen Diplomat Who Helped Secure the Soviets

The University of Washington and Winder-mere Cup have Bob Walsh—and Hall-of-Fame basketball icon Bill Russell—to thank for helping get the Soviet Union's national crew teams to the first Windermere Cup.

Walsh was born in 1940 in Winthrop, Massachusetts, just outside Boston. He graduated from Ohio's Marietta College with a degree in radio, television, and journalism. In 1967 he became a program director in Los Angeles for KABC radio. Two years later he hired Russell for a show at the station.

In 1973 the Seattle SuperSonics of the National Basketball Association hired Russell, the dominant center for NBA-dynasty the Boston Celtics during the '60s, to be their coach and general manager. He brought Walsh with him to Seattle to be his assistant GM.

Walsh left the Sonics in 1977. He became an agent and marketer who put on major sporting events in Seattle.

One of those events was the 1984 NCAA men's basketball championship in the Kingdome, the first time the "Final Four" was held in Seattle since 1952 and '49 at UW's Hec Edmundson Pavilion. Another was the 1990 Goodwill Games, a sporting and cultural exchange between the Soviet Union, the United States, and their respective allies. Cable-television tycoon Ted Turner had started the

Goodwill Games in 1986 as a response to the US-led boycott of the 1980 Moscow Olympics and the reciprocal USSR boycott of the '84 Games in Los Angeles.

Walsh had so much guile and pull with the Soviets that he received the Supreme Soviet Award from Mikhail Gorbachev, the general secretary of the Communist Party, in 1988. Presidents Ronald Reagan and George H. W. Bush were, at the time, the other Americans besides Walsh to have received the Supreme Soviet Award. Walsh received the honor for his work with the Goodwill Games in addition to his efforts in getting the first aid from western nations to the Soviet Union following a devastating earthquake in Armenia in

1988. The Armenian-relief missions were the first time American citizens and aircraft were allowed behind the Iron Curtain without visas since World War II.

Walsh also negotiated with the Soviets to permit his fellow Massachusetts native Lynne Cox to go on her historic, icy swim of Bering Strait between Alaska and the USSR in 1987. Walsh was the negotiator that made possible the 1990 "Peace Climb" of Mt. Everest. Seattle-area mountaineering icon Jim Whittaker led a record party of twenty Chinese, Soviet, and American climbers to Everest's summit.

All those connections became Windermere's and UW's key to opening diplomatic channels through which the Soviets agreed to race the Huskies in the first Windermere Cup in 1987.

After his success with that inaugural Cup and the Goodwill Games, Walsh coordinated with Russian entrepreneurs to launch a Soyuz spacecraft full of trade items and messages into orbit for a week. That 1992 event is believed to be the first commercial space flight in history. The capsule landed off the Washington coast and went on display in the Boeing Museum of Flight in Seattle.

Walsh established "Bob Walsh Enterprises" in Seattle and served as a speaker and consultant on a variety of civic and citizen-diplomacy issues in the Northwest and worldwide. Into the twenty-first century, Walsh was still working behind the scenes as a citizen diplomat on issues in the United States, Russia, and the countries of the Middle East. ∎

Fitzsimons already knew all about the Opening Day Regatta and why Washington wanted to ramp up the competition. By 1987 he had become a close supporter of the UW rowing program. Twenty-six years later, the chief could still easily rattle off the names of past Husky rowers and their accomplishments: Blake Nordstrom, UW Class of 1982, who went on to become the director and president of his family's Nordstrom, Inc., department store; Al Forney, also in that class of '82, a silver medalist in the fours with coxswain at the 1984 Olympics.

The relationship with Fitzsimons was particularly useful in prepping for the Soviets' arrival for a new, expanded Opening Day Regatta. As police chief, he was officially the city's warden of all port activities. Even though Seattle was hosting Soviets during the Cold War, even though the State Department was involved, Fitzsimons didn't recall having to deploy from SPD an overwhelming security force for that first Windermere Cup.

"It's not some English soccer fans rioting," Fitzsimons said of fans on the banks of the Montlake Cut for what has become the Windermere Cup.

Yet that didn't mean this was some afterthought event for the SPD. The city's harbor-patrol unit, led then by Duane Hoekstra, planned for all five of its boats—one small chaser boat and four larger ones with hoses—to be out for Opening Day of 1987. Fitzsimons scheduled all of the harbor unit's approximately fifteen officers to be around the Montlake Cut that race day. Then there was on-lane traffic control on and around the campus, conducted by UW traffic control's John Moffett.

Ernst remembered police boats escorting the Soviets on or around the Montlake Cut each time the USSR crew was on the water for practices that week, just to ensure against a potential international incident.

"We used the utmost precaution," Fitzsimons said. "It was a political situation; there were all kinds of politics involved. I mean, we had just come out of Jimmy Carter's era when he stopped all sports with Soviets and Americans."

Hasenmiller and Green also had to work out security arrangements for the campus dormitory and dining hall that would serve the Soviets during their stay. For that they coordinated with Chief Michael Shanahan of the University of Washington Police Department and with William Kingston, director of UW's Housing and Food Services.

"It didn't get particularly complicated," Ernst said of the planning, "until we started having meetings where thirty people were sitting around a table talking about security and transportation. It was everybody: Seattle Police, State Department, Secret Service, the fire department, university officials, state officials. Everybody."

As Hasenmiller said: "We didn't want anything bad to happen when they were here, on our watch."

PREPARING A CITY FOR THE MAIN EVENT

There were many other costs beyond security built into Windermere's $30,000 budget for that first Windermere Cup. There were printing costs, such as for the purple-and-gold pennants with 1987 on them. Jacobi had four of his children distribute those, plus printed regatta programs, around Seattle ahead of that first Cup, part of a grassroots publicity campaign that supplemented the region's television, radio, and print media's coverage.

How grassroots was it? Jacobi's son John, better known as "OB," was part of the marketing effort. The resourceful teen, a junior at Seattle's Roosevelt High School, arrived at UW's docks on Union Bay and Lake Washington immediately east of Husky Stadium days before the event to pass out Windermere Cup pennants. But the number of boaters milling around, waiting for rides out to their crafts docked along the log boom beyond the Montlake Cut, struck his entrepreneurial side as a prime opportunity for profit.

The seventeen-year-old OB Jacobi got a thirteen-foot whaler and began offering personal ferry service out to the boats. One of the people he took out to the log boom was the owner of the company that produced Normandy Rose blue jeans, an early 1980s trend of denim with snap pockets with a rose on the back.

"He gave me fifty bucks. I thought I'd died and gone to heaven," OB said decades later. "He said, 'I'm going to send you a box of jeans.' And he did! I got a box of Normandy Rose jeans. It was the best day ever...I was like, 'This is the best job ever!'"

The list of planners and organizers for that first Windermere-sponsored regatta in 1987 seemed as long as the race

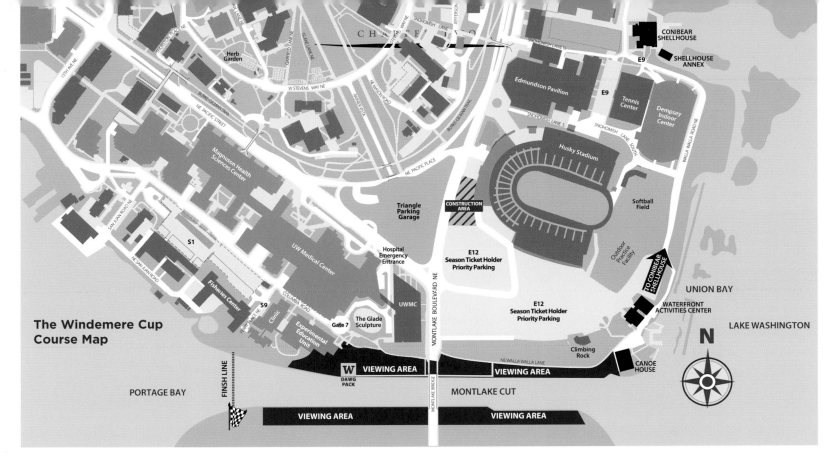

The Windemere Cup Course Map

FINISH LINE · PORTAGE BAY · DAWG PACK · W VIEWING AREA · VIEWING AREA · VIEWING AREA · VIEWING AREA · MONTLAKE CUT · MONTLAKE BRIDGE · NE WALLA WALLA LANE · Climbing Rock · CANOE HOUSE · WATERFRONT ACTIVITIES CENTER · UNION BAY · LAKE WASHINGTON · N

course: the State Department; Windermere's marketing and finance departments, led by Jim Shapiro with help from independent PR contractor John Kernell; Windermere's public-relations staff, including Lisa DeAmicis; plus the PR people at the SYC; a private tugboat operator to put in extra logs for an expanded boom to handle the anticipated larger boat crowd lining the eastern edge of the Cut; UW's transportation office and motor pool for the use of rental vans; local "hostesses" to plan the various banquets, outings, and other social functions during the Soviets' visit; the hiring of two officials from FISA, rowing's international governing body, to certify the Montlake Cut course and officiate the races.

Ernst ended up getting two FISA officials from California for the first Cup, Paul Ryan of Newport Beach and Bob Scurria from Oakland. They came at a cost of $750 in airfare, food, and lodging.

The largest expense was paid by Windermere through the "Seattle Organizing Committee," which paid the thousands of dollars per airline ticket for the approximately two dozen Soviet men and women rowers, plus the government officials

This map of the Windermere Cup race course reflects the narrow path rowers travel through the Montlake Cut to reach the finish line.

who accompanied them to Seattle.

The Soviet contingent arrived via Aeroflot at Dulles International Airport outside Washington, D.C., on the morning of April 28, 1987. Representatives of Walsh's Goodwill Games company met the group there to coordinate its passing through customs and then transfer by bus to National Airport along the Potomac River, approximately a half-hour away.

They were among the rare Soviet citizens at the time to board a US domestic flight: Northwest Airlines Flight 581 from Washington-National to Seattle-Tacoma International Airport.

Jacobi's dream for an annual grand Windermere Cup was about to become reality.

BEGINNING A LEGACY

"It was great to have the Soviets for the first [Cup]. It was a world event," Lude said. "And with Bob's connections we've had crews from Australia, New Zealand, Great Britain, the Balkan states, Italy...all of them come to Washington to race in the Windermere Cup. We didn't know if we'd have John's support beyond the first year, but after that first one, he was so excited it was easy to get his blessing for the second year."

And the third. And the fourth, the fifth...the twenty-eighth.

"As long as he's upstairs in that office at Windermere, no one else will sponsor and put on this race," Lude said.

By the thirtieth anniversary race in 2016, John Jacobi's kids were at the Windermere helm and carrying on his tradition of staging the showcase every first Saturday in May.

Through its partner, Windermere, Washington realized it had struck gold. And the Husky athletic department basked a bit in the accomplishment.

"There are not enough superlatives to express our feelings of the great job you did with the recent 'Soviet Project,'" Erickson and Ernst wrote in a May 14, 1987 letter to Green. "Your presence at their arrival (12:30 a.m.) and their departure (again, 12:30 a.m.) was important and noticed. We thought only us coaches were supposed to have that kind of endurance...We believe the entire project was a success."

In a department congratulatory letter signed by Erickson and Ernst dated that same day, the coaches thanked Hasenmiller for her ability to "anticipate."

"We want to personally thank you for the super job you did for what we will call the 'Soviet Project,'" the letter to Hasenmiller began. "Your contacts with the Bob Walsh Associates, SYC, Windermere Real Estate, the television producers, and the press, enabled you to provide everyone, including us, with useful information."

Rick Menti, who worked for Windermere then, drew praise for being "a very helpful liaison" between Lude and Jacobi.

Green reiterated that credit in thank-you letters to Ernst and Erickson dated May 18, 1987. To Ernst, the associate athletic director wrote, "The transportation situation almost got away from us, so I really appreciate your willingness to

The Soviets enjoy a festive yacht cruise the day before the race as they head to John W. Jacobi's home for a dinner party.

pitch in to find drivers and to drive yourself, as if you didn't have enough projects going on this spring. Many thanks for all your help in making it so successful." Green concluded, "We now have the groundwork for an excellent future for the Windermere Cup regatta."

RETURNING THE FAVOR

The first Windermere Cup had been such a success, the Soviets sought to return the hosting.

In June and again in September, the rowing federation of the USSR invited the Huskies' men's and women's crew teams to a "Moscow International Rowing Regatta" to be held June 3-7, 1988, in the Soviet capital.

The Soviet State Sports Federation sent the second invitation by telex through Walsh. The Soviets offered to pay all "staying expenses in Moscow" for the Huskies.

At the time there existed the feeling, as espoused in a *New York Times* article written April 30, 1989, that "in the current climate, athletic competition has become more comparable to a cultural exchange, rather than a metaphor for war...the Soviets also appear interested in solidifying their place in the world athletic community. This participation will enable them to obtain needed currency for their troubled economy."

For instance, by the end of the '80s, the first Soviet was playing in North America's National Hockey League: Sergei Priakin of the Calgary Flames.

"According to Monica DeHellerman," the *Times'* article stated, "whose Manhattan-based company sponsors an annual international sports business symposium, the Soviets made over one-hundred million between 1985 and 1988 in such (sports) revenues. She called this a conservative estimate."

Whatever their motivation, accepting the USSR's invitation for a rematch regatta a year after the rousing success of the first Windermere Cup would have enabled Washington's team to be the first crew in Soviet waters since that 1958 upset when the Huskies beat their hosts in the Moscow Cup.

AWAITING ANOTHER INVITATION

But Green, UW's senior associate athletic director, and Ernst advised Lude in a department memo written September 28, 1987, that "there are several conflicts which would preclude our attendance."

They cited the women's NCAA national championships June 4-5. The men were hoping to be training for the National Collegiate Rowing Championship (now called the IRA National Championship Regatta) to be held June 18, 1988. Plus, UW's final-exam week was June 6-10 that year.

So Lude enlisted Walsh to send a telex to his Goodwill Games contacts in the Soviet State Sports Committee and to the USSR rowing federation late in September 1987:

UNIVERSITY OF WASHINGTON REGRETS UNABLE TO ACCEPT INVITATION TO MOSCOW INTERNATIONAL ROWING REGATTA JUNE 1988. CONFLICT WITH UNIVERSITY EXAMINATIONS AND NATIONAL CHAMPIONSHIPS. WOULD LIKE TO ROW IN MOSCOW IN THE FALL 1988. AWAIT INVITATION.

The trip to Moscow in 1988 never happened. The next time the Huskies competed in the USSR wasn't until September 1, 2007, when UW went offseason to the Moscow Race of Champions to compete against Moscow State, Cambridge, and Oxford on the Moskva River as part of a celebration of the 860th anniversary of the founding of Moscow.

> **"** I had no idea it would grow into this. I didn't even know we'd be allowed to call it the Windermere Cup. I thought, they ww probably want to name it after some famous rower or something. **"**
>
> JOHN W. JACOBI

Lois Kipper hosted the Soviets at the first Windermere Cup, and she later became the first woman director of the Board of Racing Stewards, UW's crew support group.

There, almost two decades after the Berlin Wall came down and forty-nine years after Washington beat the Russians on their home course, the Huskies did it again.

BRINGING BACK THE NEW RUSSIANS

Windermere and the Huskies invited the former Soviet Union and its subsequent independent states back to four more Windermere Cups.

In 1992, the newly independent Lithuanians finished second to both UW's men's and women's crews. In 1996, Russia's men's team finished second to UW and its women finished third behind the winning Huskies and second-place Yale. In 2003, Belarus beat Washington and Notre Dame in the men's final of the Windermere Cup, and in 2006, the Russian Rowing Federation's men's and women's teams won the Windermere Cup.

All this started from Jacobi reading Newnham's column in the Sunday paper, the Windermere chief going to Erickson and Ernst the next day, and the coaches going to UW athletic director Lude to carry the first, grand Windermere Cup from idea to ideal in twelve months. "It was a dream that became a reality, because it went great," Lude said. "All of the credit to Bob and to Dick. The rest of it—all I had to do was convince people." ■

This photo of a 1924 UW men's crew rowing on Lake Washington, with Mt. Rainier making an appearance in the background, was taken long before Seattle built the Evergreen Point Floating Bridge (SR 520) to span these waters. Note this same image was used in the facing 2003 Windermere Cup poster.

Drawing from Seattle's Rowing Legacy

2003 poster

I T ' S N O T by accident that the Windermere Cup has thrived and developed into an internationally renowned crew event in the Pacific Northwest.

The region has been an innovative champion of rowing since before 1911.

That was the year George and Dick Pocock sailed by the Scottish steamer, the *Tunisian*, from Liverpool, England, to Halifax, Nova Scotia, and then took a week-long ride on the Canadian Pacific Railway from Montreal to Vancouver, British Columbia, Canada.

Within months of arriving in B.C., the Pocock brothers, whose father and grandfather built boats along the River Thames, were building racing shells for the Vancouver Rowing Club.

Hiram Conibear, then the University of Washington's rowing coach and now the man whose name is on the Huskies' impressive boathouse, learned through rowing circles of these British brothers and their shell building.

Conibear, the "Father of Washington Crew," was a native of Illinois and former trainer for track and football at the University of Chicago.

In 1906, while a trainer for baseball's Chicago White Sox, Conibear met medical student Bill Speidel. Speidel had been the Huskies' quarterback and football team captain in 1903, and linked Conibear to his contacts in the UW athletic trainers' office.

Conibear arrived in Washington in 1906 as a Huskies athletics trainer. While he and UW athletics manager Lorin Grinstead were watching a Huskies' football practice, Grinstead said in passing how desperate Washington was for a coach to lead its new crew program.

"I'd make a good one," Conibear told Grinstead, as recounted in Jim Daves' and W. Thomas Porter's 2000 book *The Glory of Washington*.

"[But] to tell you the truth, I don't know one end of the boat from another."

"To tell you the truth, I don't know one end of the boat from another."

HIRAM CONIBEAR

BUILDING A BETTER BOAT

Through library books Conibear studied the sport, and in 1907 he accepted the job as Washington's crew coach.

In 1911, upon hearing the Pococks were building shells up in Canada, Conibear traveled the 150 miles north from Seattle to Vancouver. He rowed out to the Pococks' floating shop in Coal Harbour, located on Burrard Inlet between downtown and Vancouver's Stanley Park.

Conibear offered the Pococks the job of building twelve new racing shells for the Huskies' eight-year-old rowing program. The brothers agreed to visit UW in the summer of 1912. As a boat-building home, Conibear offered the Pococks the Tokio Café, which had been built on the edge of Portage Bay near Lake Union, beyond the west edge of the UW campus, for the 1909 Alaska-Yukon-Pacific Expedition. At the time, the Huskies' varsity crew house was the US Lifesaving Station on Lake Union.

The Englishmen weren't overly impressed, but they agreed to build Conibear twelve boats for the Huskies. Problem was, the UW coach was only able to secure initial funding for one.

Dick Pocock and his father, Aaron Pocock, who by now had sailed from England to join his sons in the Northwest, moved from Vancouver to Seattle to build the *Rogers*, named for William H. Rogers, the owner of the Seattle candy and ice-cream company that donated $200 to build the Huskies' new shell in 1912.

Conibear's growing program with the Pococks' custom

University of Washington head crew coach Hiram (HB) Conibear, ca. 1907-1917, for whom UW's modern Conibear Shellhouse was named.

boats attracted the attention of the Intercollegiate Rowing Association.

In 1913 the IRA invited Conibear and the Huskies out to the Hudson River in Poughkeepsie, New York, as the first crew from the West to compete in the IRA's annual regatta. Once the UW and then California participated, the IRAs became the de facto national championships of college rowing.

PASSING THE TORCH

In 1917, just as the program he created was taking off, Conibear died from injuries sustained when falling out of a tree in his yard.

Ed Leader, who rowed for Conibear at UW, replaced him as the Huskies' coach. But in 1922 Yale offered Leader its head rowing job. Leader accepted and tried to bring George Pocock with him.

That same year George had gotten married in Seattle and had, like his siblings, just gained US citizenship. He chose to stay in Washington state. Dick Pocock took Leader's offer instead, and moved east to begin building racing boats for Yale.

By 1926, Washington had won three IRA national titles in four years under coach Rusty Callow, who had rowed for Conibear from 1914-15. When Callow left to coach Pennsylvania, the no-nonsense, suit-and-tie coach and UW alumnus Al Ulbrickson took over the Huskies. That was the fall of 1927. He furthered the foundation for the legacy George Pocock and Husky rowers have passed down through a century of excellence at UW.

"It's a great art, is rowing," begins Pocock's famous quote

on the sport he helped grow in the early 1900s. "It's the finest art there is. It's a symphony of motion, and when you're rowing well, why, it's nearing perfection. You're touching the divine. It touches the you of yous, which is your soul."

Michael Callahan won four Pacific-10 Conference championships rowing for the Huskies in the 1990s. He won two Under 23 world championships for the United States in 1995 and '96.

Then, after a stint at *Bloomberg News* in New Jersey while training with the national rowing team, Callahan accepted

UW director of rowing Bob Ernst's offer to be his assistant coach in 2004.

A decade later, he was winning the first of five IRA national titles in seven years with the Huskies. "An unwavering work ethic is at the core of our ethos at Washington," Callahan said in 2013, in the midst of Washington winning three consecutive national titles. "Competition and commitment is our foundation."

That ethos, and the international stature it has created, have roots that stretch back to one of the University of

The Man Who Revived the Story of UW's 1936 Olympians

Had Joe Rantz's daughter not liked to read, and not liked books written by Daniel James Brown, UW's 1936 "boys in the boat" might not have become so wildly popular as they did again in the twenty-first century.

Judy Willman had brought home a previous book of Brown's to her father. Joe Rantz lived with his daughter for the last years of his life. That house was next door to Brown's in the Seattle suburb of Redmond, Washington.

Often in 2007, the neighbors stopped to chat. Willman told Brown he really ought to talk to her father, Rantz, about his life.

"The more he talked, the more intrigued and fascinated I became," Brown said. "After two hours of talking to him, I was absolutely hooked."

That interview spurred Brown to write the bestselling book, *The Boys in the Boat*.

Brown was born in 1951 in Berkeley, California. He attended Diablo

Valley College east of Berkeley and then the University of California, Washington's rowing archrival, in his hometown. He taught writing at San Jose State University and Stanford before becoming a technical writer and editor.

His own family history led him to write one of his first acclaimed nonfiction books, *Under a Flaming Red Sky*. He investigated the fire that on September 1, 1894, destroyed the town of Hinckley, Minnesota, shattered his grandfather's life there, and killed his great-grandfather. That book was a finalist for a Washington State Book Award in 2007, the same year Willman told Brown about her father and the 1936 Husky crew that shocked Hitler and the world by winning gold at the Berlin Games.

Brown also wrote *The Indifferent Stars Above*, the story of a young bride who left her home in Illinois in the spring of 1846 to travel to California. Sarah Graves and her new spouse joined the infamous Donner Party and its tragic travels through California's Sierra Nevada Mountains.

Brown's five-acre property in Redmond was a reminder of Rantz and *The Boys in the Boat*. That's because in retirement, the ever-charging Rantz made posts and other wooden products from cedar.

"He made another living finding old cedar logs and dragging them out of the forest," Brown said, marveling at Rantz for his life determination and craftsmanship, as well as his rowing. "He hand-split the rails and posts for the cedar fence in my backyard." ∎

Washington's greatest athletic accomplishments, the "boys in the boat" legacy.

LIVING A LEGACY

The 1936 Washington's men's varsity eight completed perhaps the greatest race ever rowed by an American crew. It was so grand, it became the basis for a best-selling book in 2013 by Daniel James Brown, *The Boys in the Boat*, that was also optioned to be produced into a movie.

The '36 Huskies, in their latest wooden Pocock shell of the time, the Husky Clipper, shocked their host Germans, the co-favorite Italians, and the world to win Olympic gold in front of Adolph Hitler at the Berlin Games.

Brown's fellow author David Laskin called Brown's story of UW's steel-minded rowers hardened by the Great Depression becoming international heroes a "Chariots of Fire with oars."

Rantz was born in Spokane. His mother died when he was three. At the start of the Great Depression, when Rantz was fifteen, his father and stepmother moved the rest of the family and left Joe on his own in Sequim on Washington's Olympic Peninsula, where he began high school.

He spent three years fending for himself, often living with strangers, until an uncle brought Joe to Seattle's Roosevelt High School for his senior year. There, Joe competed for the gymnastics team. Rantz's athleticism on the bars at Roosevelt attracted Ulbrickson, the Washington crew coach whose campus was a mile and a half from the high school.

That figures; the best crew coaches are notorious for finding ultra-athletic and competitive rowers from many other sports. UW rowing coaches Callahan and Ernst have said they regularly attend the Washington state high school basketball and volleyball championships to find the rugged, determined athletes who they feel they can mold into Husky rowers.

Enjoying the 2012 Windermere Cup from the Conibear Shellhouse balcony is legendary Stan R. Pocock (1923-2014), a former rower and coach for UW. He also coached several US men's crews to gold in the Olympics (1956 and 1960). In 2012, Pocock received the Medal of Honor Award from USRowing, their lifetime achievement award.

"In rowing, it's not like soccer where the kid has been competing in it since he was four and you can identify the kid. You are recruiting on physiology," Callahan said. "A lot of kids end up switching sports, say from football to rowing, and they might have a great physiological gift—lung capacity or what have you. We're looking for personality types. Are you competitive? Do you have a really strong work ethic? So we identify people early and also pretty late, too."

Rantz's physical gifts seventy years ago earned the Roosevelt High gymnast a spot on UW's varsity boat in his sophomore season.

That's how Joe Rantz became a Husky—and then an Olympic champion as one of the boys in the boat.

Willman, Rantz's daughter, recalls that Ulbrickson kept trying to demote her father because the new rower's form was inconsistent, "but every time [Ulbrickson] replaced him with someone else, the boat slowed down."

Rantz was the last man selected for the varsity eight boat in 1936.

That was no small feat, as those Huskies were no novices on the water. They had already won three national championships within a decade by the time Rantz got to Washington in the mid-1930s. Yet he got right into the seven seat in the varsity eight.

Rantz never lost a race as a Husky. He paid his way through UW working summer jobs, such as laboring on the Grand Coulee Dam in broiling, Eastern Washington heat. Such work hardened him for the 1936 Olympics and, ultimately, for the gold-medal race in front of Hitler and his Nazis at the Berlin Games.

WOWING THE WORLD

Rantz. Don Hume. George E. Hunt. James B. McMillin. John G. White. Gordon B. Adam. Charles Day. Roger Morris. And coxswain Robert G. Moch.

Those sons of loggers, shipyard

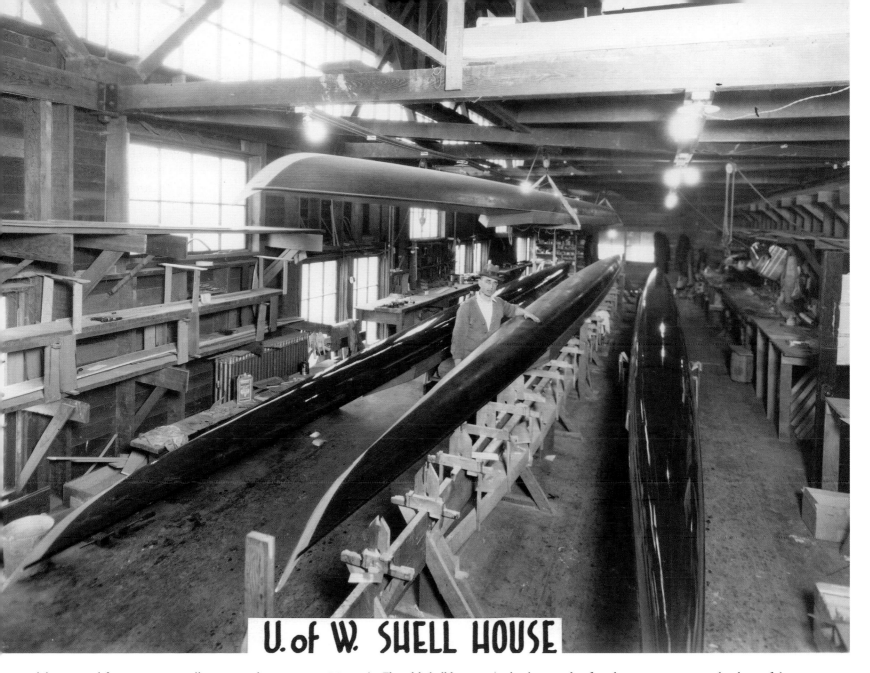

U. of W. SHELL HOUSE

The old shell house for UW, containing several boats built by the Pocock brothers.

laborers and farmers—now college guys who swept out Hec Edmundson Pavilion after UW basketball and track events to earn cash for lunch—won the 1936 IRAs by beating archrival California, ending the Bears' streak of three consecutive national championships. The Huskies then beat the best of the upper-crusters in the Ivy League. They ultimately beat everyone in the country to become the United States' rowing team for the Berlin Games.

Brown (a graduate of Cal, by the way) wrote Washington's 1936 story in *The Boys in the Boat* as much about the unique backgrounds of its dominant rowers as he does of their victory over the world as Olympic upstarts.

"They were Westerners. They grew up in logging camps and on farms. They were pretty tough," Brown said. "They weren't sons of bankers or lawyers, like many of the East Coast kids they rowed against. They were self-sufficient, for sure.

"They went through this vigorous process just to become U-Dub's team. A couple hundred boys showed up at Washington to try out for the rowing team that year. There was this intense bonding factor that helped make them so good as a team."

Yet they almost didn't go to Berlin.

It took an eleventh-hour, grassroots fundraising campaign across Washington after the US Olympic trials to raise $5,000 to pay the Huskies' way from New York to Germany by steamship.

Those Berlin Games remain known for Jesse Owens wowing Hitler on the track. On August 14, 1936, those Huskies did the same thing on the water.

For the Olympic finals, the Huskies were left in lane six on the outside of the blustery Lake Grunau course, just twenty miles south of Berlin. The race began with the UW boat still stationary as its competitors sped away. From their distant lane, the Huskies couldn't hear the starting signal over the wind rippling across the lake or over the noise of 70,000 fans that included Hitler and his top Nazi aides.

"Let's get out of here! The race has started!" Rantz reportedly yelled from inside the UW boat.

Washington was still dead last at the 1,000-meter mark, halfway through the race.

But then the Huskies zoomed at forty-four strokes per minute, faster than they had ever rowed. The Huskies passed Great Britain, Hungary, Switzerland, and Germany. Then they passed the stunned Italians in the race's final ten strokes.

The Huskies finished their rally from gummed-up to gold in 6:25.4, a world and Olympic record for an eight-man boat over 2,000 meters.

And they needed every stroke to do it. Washington won by a mere six-tenths of a second.

CARRYING ON THE TRADITION

Rantz and his teammates returned to UW as national heroes.

Rantz won big off the water, too. On the same day he graduated in 1939 with a chemical engineering degree from UW, he married Joyce Simdars. They raised a family of five in the Seattle suburb of Lake Forest Park. For thirty-five years

> ## " They weren't sons of bankers or lawyers, like many of the East Coast kids they rowed against. They were self-sufficient, for sure. "
>
> DANIEL JAMES BROWN

The men of *The Boys in the Boat* fame who won gold in the 1936 Berlin Olympics. From left to right: Roger Morris, bow; Charles Day, no. 2; Gordon B. Adam, no. 3; John G. White, no. 4; James B. McMillin, no. 5; George E. Hunt, no. 6; Joseph Rantz, no. 7; Don B. Hume, stroke; and Robert G. Moch, coxswain, crouching in front.

Rantz was a chemical engineer at Boeing. He is credited with contributing to the invention of a dust-free workspace known as a "safe room."

In 1970, Rantz and the Huskies' gold medalists were inducted into the USA National Rowing Hall of Fame. In 1979, the UW established its Husky Hall of Fame and honored those golden 1936 rowers among its earliest members.

During retirement, the ever-charging Rantz made posts and other wooden products from cedar. By now it may not surprise you that he didn't simply whittle wood sharps someone fetched for him. "He made another living out of finding old cedar logs and dragging them out of the forest," Brown said, marveling at Rantz beyond his rowing heroism. "He hand-split the rails and posts for the cedar fence in my backyard."

A few months after Brown completed his series of wowing interviews with Rantz for the book, Rantz died of natural causes at his daughter's home in September of 2007. He was ninety-three, and one of the last remaining rowers from that golden UW moment.

Brown used documentations the children, and in one case a nephew, of Rantz's teammates kept of their fathers' gold-medal experiences to give *The Boys in the Boat* its depth of details.

Brown included in his promotional works some film footage of the Huskies' victory at the Berlin Games. That came from Leni Riefenstahl, the German film producer who became Hitler's favorite filmmaker.

"We started here before professional sports developed," Callahan said of Husky crew, a few feet from where UW's 1936 Olympic-winning shell hangs inside Washington's Conibear Shellhouse. "And we've been able to carry it on." ■

The one and only Windermere Cup trophy, a crystal punchbowl that weighs fourteen pounds, holds about three gallons, and was worth $12,000 when created in 1987 for the inaugural regatta.

The Making
of a Legacy Trophy

2006 poster

THE DESIGN of the Windermere Cup regatta trophy comes from links that stretch back to the mid-twentieth century.

Rick Menti had known John Jacobi since 1958, when they were pledge brothers in a UW fraternity. "We were fast friends," Menti said of Jacobi. "Ultimately, my wife (Patti) went to work for him."

So did he. By 1987, Rick Menti, son of Harlan "Huck" and Torborg "Torb" Menti, founders of Menti Jewelers in Moses Lake, Washington, had minor ownership interests in some Windermere Real Estate offices in the south Puget Sound.

Jacobi knew Menti's family owned a jewelry store, so as plans gained momentum for the first Windermere Cup, he and Mike Lude, then Huskies' athletic director, called Menti.

"He had this concept for a bigger, international race. And he wanted a bigger grand trophy," said Menti, an active mem-ber of the UW's Tyee Club of boosters at the time. "So I talked to Mike about it, and I was kind of a matchmaker for them and the jewelry business."

Through the jewelry business, Menti's parents were good friends with the parents of Anton C. "Chuck" Kusak III, chief and heir of Kusak Cut Glass Works of Seattle.

So Menti asked Kusak to design and commission the trophy for the new regatta.

ENLISTING THE BEST
FOR THE BEST

"This was a big deal," Kusak said. "The Soviets were coming for that first Windermere Cup. Mr. Jacobi said he wanted a grand trophy to commemorate this grand event.

"I told him, 'I think I have something that will be pretty spectacular for you.' At the time, there weren't many big pieces of crystal like what we came up with."

Kusak Cut Glass Works, founded in 1914, became one of America's premier crystal companies. In 1986 it had an eight-liter crystal punch bowl with a wooden base. Kusak sketched designs of a window for the front of the cup, an uncut place on which an engraved Windermere Cup "plaque" could be displayed. He sent those designs to Bohemia Crystal Glass in Sazava, Czechoslovakia, located in the central Bohemian region of that Soviet-bloc nation.

> " It is truly one of the finest pieces of crystal Kusak Cut Glass Works has produced in our hundred-year history…It turned out beautifully, and so the trophy was born. "
>
> CHUCK KUSAK

"I had the punch bowl," Kusak said. "But I had to have one made with a window on it so I could do the engraving."

Kusak's enjoyed what is believed to be America's longest, sustained family history with the famed Czech glass industry. Chuck Kusak's grandfather, Anton C. Kusak, Sr., apprenticed at a crystal factory in Czechoslovakia back in 1906, eight years before he opened Kusak Cut Glass Works in Seattle.

So in 1987, Kusak Cut Glass Works sent its bowl to

Rowers receive medals for placing in the Dick Erickson Memorial Cascade Cup, which is also held on Opening Day.

MEN'S WINDEMERE CUP RESULTS

	FIRST	SECOND	THIRD
2015	New Zealand	Washington	Columbia
2014	Great Britain	Washington	
2013	Washington	Cornell	Dartmouth
2012	Washington	Argentina	Virginia
2011	Washington	Stanford	Cambridge
2010	Washington	Syracuse	Oxford
2009	Washington	Oregon State	Brazil
2008	Washington	Poland	Naval Academy
2007	Washington	Purdue	Waikato University-New Zealand
2006	Russian National Team	Washington	Michigan
2005	Washington	Czech Republic	Cornell
2004	Washington	Navy	Italy
2003	Washington	Northeastern	Poland
2002	Washington	Stanford	China
2001	Croatian Olympic Team	University of Victoria	Washington
2000	Washington	Navy	Egyptian National Team
1999	Washington	New Zealand National Team	
1998	Washington	Nottinghamshire County Rowing	
1997	Washington	Australian National Team	
1996	Washington	Yale	Russian National Team
1995	Washington	South Africa	
1994	Washington	Dutch National Team	Stanford
1993	Washington	Dartmouth	Humboldt (Germany)
1992	Washington	Lithuania	Cambridge
1991	Washington	Cornell	Czechoslovakia
1990	People's Republic of China	Navy	Washington
1989	Italy	Washington	New Zealand
1988	Australia	Washington	Princeton
1987	Soviet Union	Washington	

Bohemia Crystal Glass to put those Windermere Cup trophy designs into production. The Bohemian craftsmen then hand blew and hand cut the full lead crystal into the Windermere Cup.

Kusak couldn't order just one cup; he had to order twenty-five trophies, the industry standard for commissioning custom pieces. But Windermere needed only one cup. (What happened with the other twenty-four is unknown.) The Windermere Cup is a perpetual trophy presented each year to the race's winning team, then inscribed with the champion's name.

"It is truly one of the finest pieces of crystal Kusak Cut Glass Works has produced in our hundred-year history," Kusak said. "It turned out beautifully, and so the trophy was born."

REWARDING MORE THAN ATHLETES

The Windermere Cup trophy—from the bottom of its wooden base to the top of the glass cup—sits thirteen inches high and is eleven inches in diameter. The trophy weighs fourteen pounds and the cup itself holds close to three gallons.

Kusak estimated the Windermere Cup was worth $12,000 when created in 1987. The trophy is displayed outside the athletes' dining room of the Conibear Shellhouse in a see-through rectangular case, so it's visible year-round.

The cup was unusual at that time, explained Kusak, for both its size and for the fact that its designer was traditionally known for "hearth-and-home" products. But the glass market was evolving, and newer generations didn't buy as much crystal for their homes. The timing of Kusak's first sports trophy, plus how well the Windermere Cup trophy was received, gave Kusak's company an ideal segue into a new market.

"The Windermere Cup is how we got into the trophy business," Kusak said. "Now we do trophies all across the country. We've gotten really big into golf awards, and we have a really strong business with the Los Angeles Yacht Club."

The winners' names for each year's men's and women's final race are engraved on plaques attached to the cup's wooden base. Following the final races, winning teams are photographed with the trophy back on the docks of the Conibear Shellhouse .

Since 2013, Windermere Cup winners also receive hand-blown glass medals in a color corresponding to how they placed in the race: gold for first, white for the traditional silver second place, and cobalt blue for third place. The image of the Windermere Cup crystal trophy is embossed into a glass medallion and is encircled with the "Windermere Cup regatta" name.

Local artist Tracy Vaughn, a former Windermere agent, made the medallions. The Washington native and busy mom of two also taught spin cycle classes while spending a decade fundraising for the Pilchuck Glass School.

Menti's wife, Patti, was part of the Windermere planning team for that first Cup in 1987, after which the Soviets' names were the first engraved onto the new trophy. As of 2012, Patti was still volunteering for the event.

"It really is a special event for a lot of the agents," Rick Menti said. "It's an opportunity for us to share some Windermere spirit with them, through the Windermere Cup."

For that first regatta and past its twenty-fifth anniversary, the Mentis enjoyed watching the race from a boat set along the log boom near the Montlake Cut, cheering crews from all over the world and seeing close up who wins the trophy Rick helped to create. ∎

Photo: Scott Eklund/Red Box Pictures

WOMEN'S WINDEMERE CUP RESULTS

	FIRST	SECOND	THIRD
2015	Washington	Virginia	
2014	Washington	Great Britain	
2013	Washington	Cornell	Dartmouth
2012	Washington	Gonzaga	Argentina
2011	Washington	Oklahoma	Cambridge
2010	Washington	Syracuse	Oxford
2009	Washington	Miami	Brazil
2008	Washington	Naval Academy	Melbourne University (Australia)
2007	Washington	Waikato University - New Zealand	Purdue
2006	Russian National Team	Washington	University of Central Florida
2005	Czech Republic	Washington	Cornell
2004	Washington	Italy	UCLA
2003	Belarus	Washington	Notre Dame
2002	Washington	Stanford	Great Britain
2001	Washington	Romania	University of Victoria
2000	Washington	Navy	Egyptian National Team
1999	Washington	Brown	New Zealand National Team
1998	British National Team	Washington	Virginia
1997	Washington	Northeastern	Australian National Team
1996	Washington	Russia	Yale
1995	Washington	South Africa	
1994	Washington	Dutch National Team	Stanford
1993	Washington	Boston	Humboldt (Germany)
1992	Washington	Lithuania	Cambridge
1991	Czechoslovakia	Cornell	Washington
1990	People's Republic of China	Cambridge	Washington
1989	New Zealand	Washington	California
1988	Washington	Australia	
1987	Soviet Union	Washington	California

LEFT: **2013 UW men's rowers, the same for which Seamus Labrum (Chapter Eleven) rowed, stuff the cup with their glass gold medals.**

LEFT:
Hand-blown, silver glass medals are bestowed upon second-place winners in the Windermere Cup regatta.

RIGHT:
OB Jacobi high-fives a female rower as rowing coach and emcee Bob Ernst watches proudly.

For the 2012 Windermere Cup women's eight race, UW hosted crews from Argentina and Gonzaga.

Blue-handled oars wait to be put into action while resting on the Conibear Shell-house pier.

Photo: Scott Eklund/Red Box Pictures

Leaving Lithuania
to Compete
in the Windermere Cup

1992 poster

ONE YEAR after Moscow finally recognized the independence of the former Soviet republic, Lithuania came to Seattle to row in the 1992 Windermere Cup. Yet Russian troops still occupied the former Soviet republic into 1993. Kestas Sereiva, one of the most respected men to row in the Windermere Cup, knew that Russian occupation harrowingly well.

By that sixth Cup in May 1992, Sereiva had completed his remarkable journey to the University of Washington and the Huskies' rowing program.

"Oh, my goodness! I had always dreamed of going to the United States to go to college," said Sereiva in early 2016 from Dover, Massachusetts, where he, his Lithuanian wife, and their three children were living while he worked as a partner at The Boston Consulting Group. "I was basically able to fulfill my dream. It wouldn't have happened without U-Dub rowing. My teammates from there remain my best

friends to this day."

Teammates such as Daniel James and Michael Doyle. They lived with Sereiva inside Conibear Shellhouse back when UW's rowing house had dormitory rooms. Doyle, from San Francisco, visited UW for the 1989 and '90 Windermere Cups and then enrolled at the university.

He was a manager for Sereiva's 1993 Huskies' rowing team. Doyle graduated from UW and eventually became a top agent in Seattle for Windermere Real Estate.

Doyle knows what Windermere founder John Jacobi meant when he said, "Kestas is one of the most impressive young people I have ever met."

Sereiva was eighteen years old in 1990, two years before that sixth Windermere Cup became the first one to host a former Soviet republic. He was hiding in his own land. Occupying Soviet troops wanted to draft the teen into their military. In March of 1990, Lithuania had become the first of the Baltic countries to declare its independence.

But the crumbling Soviet Union was fighting against the insurgency inside a nation of 3.7 million people that covers less than one-third the area of Washington.

Soviet soldiers first occupied Lithuania in 1945. They'd killed hundreds of thousands, including elite intellectuals. And 1990 proved to be the final occupation, the end of which helped accelerate the fall of the USSR in late '91.

"I would live at friends' houses," Sereiva told the *Seattle Times* in 1995, of being eighteen in Lithuania. "After almost a year of hiding, I enrolled at the university [in the capital city of Vilnius]. There was a new law that students couldn't be drafted. Still, it wasn't safe to be walking in the streets.

"The Russians were riding in military trucks and they would see a young guy walking, and they would just grab him. They would take him to a drafting center and investigate his papers. Usually those guys got beat up by Russian soldiers." Or sent to Siberia.

CASHING HIS WAY OUT

Sereiva's parents got creative—and illegal—to avoid these fates for Kestas and his older brother by two years, Gintaras. In the late 1980s their mother and father visited an uncle who was living in Chicago. They brought back to Lithuania two American VCRs, which were a forbidden luxuries in the Communist world. In 1991 his parents sold one of the VCRs on the Lithuanian black market. That money bought Kestas his new life in the form of a plane ticket for his brother and himself to visit that uncle in Chicago.

Bob Ernst, Sereiva's rowing coach at UW, remembered of Kestas' arrival in the United States: "All he had was a Soviet passport, basically."

"That, and one hundred dollars," Sereiva said.

The Sereiva brothers' trek to the US included a torturously long wait in lines at the Moscow airport. Soviet authorities

> " He spoke at a Windermere Cup event about his background and the role rowing played in making him who he is today. It brought me to tears. He's one of the finest people I've ever met. "
>
> JOHN W. JACOBI

Rowers enjoy a misty sunrise over Lake Washington as morning commuters snake along the SR 520 bridge toward downtown Seattle.

there checked documentation for hours before finally deciding to let Kestas and his brother continue on to Chicago.

Gintaras, a standout soccer player, eventually returned to the newly independent Lithuania, but Kestas stayed in Illinois. He found yard work to make money. One of his jobs was for commercial photographer Leslie Hicks and her husband, Ed, a commercial pilot.

The Hicks helped Kestas get other yard-work jobs and learn the English language. One day Sereiva needed a new dress shirt to attend a wedding party in Illinois. Leslie Hicks took him to a men's store but couldn't find a shirt that fit him.

"Wow, your arms seem unusually long," Hicks told Sereiva.

"Yeah," Kestas joked, "they stretched from rowing."

That's how his American host family learned Sereiva had rowed for Lithuania's junior national team before his escape to the US.

The Hicks' twenty-year-old son at the time was a film student at the University of Southern California, so USC was the first US university rowing program to which Leslie Hicks wrote a letter on behalf of Sereiva. She figured rowing was a way to get Kestas a student visa for a longer, legal stay in the US.

In 1991, USC's program was slowly growing, a club sport that didn't offer scholarships. But in a stroke of luck for the Lithuanian, the Trojans' coach at the time, Dave Nesbit, had rowed in 1985 and '86 for Ernst at Washington.

"Why don't you go somewhere that has an established rowing program?" Nesbit asked Hicks and Sereiva. He had Ernst's phone number handy, and that's how Sereiva found one of the nation's top rowing programs, sight unseen—and vice versa.

Sereiva didn't know the language. He remembered his college entrance exam scores: in the twentieth percentile for English but the ninety-ninth percentile for math. Yet he had an unmistakable determination and maturity—plus, an incredible back story.

Photo: Joel W. Rogers Photography

"I invest, number one, in somebody who is bulletproof with his or her character," Ernst said, "and number two, someone who works really, really hard."

Sereiva was all that. And more.

"Kestas," Ernst said in 2016, "is a really unique story."

Once in Seattle, Sereiva gravitated toward computer science. He also continued his yard work—for John Jacobi.

At the time the Windermere head man was building a home on Bainbridge Island across Elliott Bay from Seattle. Jacobi hired the young Husky rower to work there.

All summer Sereiva would row with the Huskies in morning workouts on the UW campus. He couldn't afford a car, nor did he want to borrow one because of the more expensive ferry toll for it, so after practice he would ride a bike about five miles through downtown traffic to Seattle's ferry terminal. There he would board a boat to Bainbridge Island, then bike five or so more miles across the island to Jacobi's property. He made this round trip each work day, mornings and evenings.

To save more money, Ernst recalls Sereiva living in the garage of Jeanne (Grainger) Hasenmiller. The former UW rower and Huskies' assistant sports information director was, by 1992, vice president for marketing and communications for Windermere. For a time Sereiva also did yard work around the house of Nordstrom department-store co-president Blake Nordstrom and his wife, Molly.

Sereiva lived some of those UW summers in Jacobi's new guest house he helped build on Bainbridge Island.

As Jacobi watched Sereiva bike to and from his place each day to work, he would marvel, "That guy's got some unbelievable determination."

"John was just so impressed that he was doing all this to get his education and succeed," Ernst said.

PROVING HIS LOYALTY

That wasn't as easy as it may have looked. Holidays and those summers were Sereiva's toughest times emotionally. He missed his family, his food, and his Lithuanian culture that was half a world away.

"In the summers everyone else went home to their families. I was in Seattle by myself," he said. "Those were the dodgy moments I thought of giving up and going home.

"To be able to have John and his wife, Roz, make me feel at home, was incredible. They were always so supportive. They got me through it.

"I will always be incredibly appreciative of what they did for me."

On the water, Ernst promoted Sereiva from junior varsity to varsity in 1992, during the Lithuanian's first year at UW. That year the Huskies routed his native national team by almost thirteen seconds in the men's final of the Windermere Cup.

But after the first race of the '93 season, Sereiva, whom Ernst said had a "funky" stroke which needed correcting, herniated a disk in his back. He didn't row for nearly two years. Yet in an indication of the impression he'd made upon them, his Huskies' teammates still voted him as the team's commodore, the leader of the student-led organization of rowers, for the fall and winter quarters of crew's offseason.

He healed and was the three seat on the Huskies' varsity eight on May 6, 1995, when Washington hosted its first African nation for a Windermere Cup. Sereiva and the undefeated Huskies routed South Africa by more than twelve seconds that day.

Sereiva graduated the following spring with a degree in computer science. Ernst had stressed to him the importance of picking an employer that would help him obtain a work visa through the US government, and perhaps eventually a green card, granting the foreign national permanent residency. To do that, the coach advised the Lithuanian he would need to stay with his first employer for at least two years, to give a commitment not to jump to a better-paying job before then.

Sereiva's character proved as strong as his word.

He stayed with Aspen Technology for not two or three, but nine years, from just after UW graduation in 1996 until the summer of 2005. He rose from software developer through consultant, senior consultant and advisor to business consultant. In August 2005 Sereiva joined The Boston Consulting Group. The global management consulting firm, by early 2016, had eighty-two offices in forty-six countries.

In May 2007 he earned a master's of business administration degree from the Tuck School of Business at Dartmouth. After rising to the position of principal at The Boston Consulting Group in 2011 at its Boston office, Sereiva returned to UW. He was the keynote speaker for the athletes' dinner before the 25th Windermere Cup in 2011.

"He married a Lithuanian girl. They have beautiful, blonde, Lithuanian poster-children," Ernst said. "He's made it. And he is one of the nicest people on the face of the earth."

Sereiva felt the same way about Ernst.

"He really improved my life," Sereiva said of his Huskies coach. "I came to U-Dub a teenager living without his parents anywhere near, not sure who I can trust. And he stuck with me. I injured my back and my first time back on the erg machine in almost two years I was dead last on the team. And he stuck through that with me."

Sereiva said a life lesson Ernst taught him while he and the Huskies were packing up equipment following a regatta in San Diego stayed with him more than twenty years later.

"We were using duct tape and I just wrapped up the boat quickly," Sereiva said. "And Bob came up to me and said, 'The tape is wrinkled.' I thought, 'You've got to be kidding

UW women's eight celebrates its victory over Virginia in the 2015 Windermere Cup regatta.

me!' But he said, 'Kestas, never do things—even little things—in any way but the right way.'

"He taught me that excellence in life is about perfection in every detail."

Yes, the man who hid as a teen in his homeland from Soviet troops, who used a black-market VCR to get to the US, then did yard work to stay, credits his rowing experience of three Windermere Cups and four years at UW with succeeding in his new world.

"Rowing really requires a ton of character and a ton of work," Sereiva said. "You know, it takes so many hours and so many strokes to prepare for and to win a race. It's delayed gratification with a lot of hard work."

Sereiva said he and his UW teammates conducted a study that found 2,000 or more minutes of practice went into each minute of race rowing.

"It's not like in basketball, where you score so much during a game," he said of rowing. "It's just you and your teammates constantly chipping away.

"And in rowing, unless you are in a single, you are learning to be a dependable person. Number one, you have to show up. And you have to be ready. It doesn't matter if you are sick or it's 5 a.m., the rest of the boat is counting on you. If one person is performing 10 percent less than his best, it affects the entire boat. You can't have 'off' days."

More than twenty years after he last rowed for UW, Sereiva still admired by Jacobi.

"In all the years that I've employed people to do physical labor on projects for me, Kestas was by far the hardest working; the kid could lift a house," Windermere's founder said in early 2016. "A few years back he spoke at a Windermere Cup event about his background and the role rowing played in making him who he is today. It brought me to tears. He is one of the finest people I've ever met." ■

Rowing requires not just power and speed, but coordination with crew mates to achieve machine-like timing for each oar stroke.

Aussie! Aussie! Aussie! Upset! Upset! Upset!

THE WINDERMERE CUP

est. 1987

1997 poster

FOR THE FIRST Windermere Cup in 1987, Ernst relied on Bob Walsh, diplomacy, and other people's contacts to secure the Soviets. For most Cups after, Ernst leaned on his impressive stable of international rowing contacts.

That includes helping Windermere go Down Under to secure the Australians for the second Cup in 1988. The Aussies won that men's final by about half a second and beat UW and Princeton in the women's main event.

In 1989, Australian John Boultbee became secretary general of the International Rowing Federation (FISA). Ernst knew Boultbee from previous Olympics and stayed an acquaintance when Boultbee became director for the Australian Institute of Sport in 1995.

A year later Boultbee oversaw Australia's rowers to win sixteen medals, including six gold, at the Atlanta 1996 Sum-

mer Olympics. Ernst phoned Boultbee soon after, one call in a long line of those congratulating Australia.

But Ernst added an offer no one else could present: an invitation for Australia's men's and women's Olympic crews to row in the 1997 Windermere Cup.

"Boultbee says, 'Okay, we have guys that are in semi-training over here. We'll send that eight so they have something to do,'" Ernst said. "There were five Olympic champions in that boat."

PREPARING OLYMPIANS

Boultbee saw Ernst's invitation in 1997 as a chance to reward his Olympians. "It came at a time that was a good opportunity to showcase our Olympians," he said in early 2014 from his office in Australia. "And they were the right people to have at the Windermere Cup because of their profile. They were good representatives for our nation's rowing program."

The Australian men, like the Soviets, were older than college age. They were also the two-time Olympic champions in the men's coxless fours at the '92 and '96 Games.

Boultbee also saw the Windermere Cup as an opportunity to garner increased exposure for his Australian crew on another world stage right as the next Olympic cycle started.

That's how the Windermere Cup was viewed after just ten years in existence: an event renowned by the world's rowing community.

"Everyone knew of the Opening Day Regatta there in Seattle and the Windermere Cup; it was well-known internationally," Boultbee said. "Over the years I had seen some impressive international crews race there. I guess I was hoping our Australians would be invited at some stage."

Now the Olympic champions wanted UW and Windermere to call them, and not just for the prestige.

Historically, the best international-crew regattas had been held in Europe. Teams had to pay their own expenses to attend. "Europe expected everyone to drop everything and gravitate there to those races," Boultbee said.

Not Windermere and UW. They dropped everything on the world's best crews to get them to Seattle.

Windermere corporate funds pay about $200,000 each year to bring domestic and international teams to Seattle. Windermere buys round-trip airfare, funds teams' lodging at a hotel near UW's athletic facilities (teams used dorms on campus for the Cup's first years), feeds the racers, their coaches and entourage, even pays for promotion and awards, plus additional materials, to put on the races.

So when Ernst called Boultbee in 1996 and invited his Australian Olympians to race in the Windermere Cup, Boultbee jumped at the opportunity for exposure to a world-class regatta—an all-expense-paid regatta.

"I know most rowing federations, like ours, have a limited budget. The opportunity and the conditions for getting to the Windermere Cup made it such an attractive event."

BRACING FOR SURPRISE

Yet it was far from a perfect week for the Australians.

A few days before race day, Boultbee got to know more of Seattle than he or his women's team wanted. They learned firsthand about the renowned UW Medical Center, as

Cornell guts it out for the 2013 Windermere Cup regatta, placing second behind the Huskies (in background) and ahead of third-place winner Dartmouth.

their coxswain fell so ill that Boultbee had to take her to the emergency room.

Race day dawned with less-than-ideal weather, a not-so-rare occurrence for early May in Seattle. The Australians rowed their way from Washington's shell house past boats tied along the log booms on the east side of Union Bay. The throng was louder and closer for more of the course than they'd experienced in the Olympics the previous summer on Georgia's Lake Lanier outside Atlanta.

The veteran Aussies lined up, their shell abreast the Hus-

The cement banks of the Montlake Cut are often painted with messages to visiting crew teams.

kies' shell near the starting line for the two-boat men's final. That was the closest they got to UW the entire race.

The Huskies stole a flying start that stunned the Australians, and the visitors never recovered. Washington won going away, swamping the stunned Olympians.

"I was surprised a college crew would look that polished," said James Thompkins, one of Australia's two-time Olympic champions.

So was Ernst.

Immediately after that 1997 race capped off a perfect

"We beat 'em. I couldn't believe we beat them."

BOB ERNST

nine-for-nine sweep for UW in Windermere Cup races, Ernst told the UW *Daily* student newspaper, "Our guys managed to steal the start and they did a great job of holding it all the way. Coming in, I thought we would be lucky to come within ten seconds."

Almost twenty years later he was still calling his Huskies' win against Australia's world-class veterans the biggest upset in the event's first quarter-century. "We beat 'em. I couldn't believe we beat them," Ernst said. "We had a good team that year. We ended up being the national champions."

Australia's women's team fared even worse for the women's final.

Within the first few strokes of the race, an Aussie rower sitting mid-boat "caught a crab," a slang term for the dreaded breaking of an out-of-sync oar. At the end of the log boom, far from the Montlake Cut, Australia's women crew was finished.

Legend has it the Australians came to Seattle for a party that week, especially the older men's team, and that they found one that lasted much of their raucous week in Seattle.

"I couldn't believe we beat them. But I think they drank their eyeballs out the whole first part of the week," Ernst said, chuckling.

Boultbee, speaking decades later from Australia, denied the Aussies used that Cup week as an American spring break. "The men's crew, they were taking it seriously," Boultbee said. "We didn't see it as just a party. We saw it as an opportunity to get more training in a competitive, unique environment. The enjoyment came after the race, at the events and celebrations they held there for the crews. They were still focused on their race."

He said his guys simply lost to a better-performing crew, and that his accomplished Olympic veterans—he called them "resting Olympians" days before the race—were simply out-classed on the water by the young Huskies in the biggest upset in Windermere Cup history. "The Washington kids, they were better." ∎

UW women's crew coach Jan Harville and Australia's coach present awards together.

A young female UW rower carrying her oars back to the Conibear Shellhouse after winning the 2015 Windermere Cup.

How the Cup Changed Jenni Hogan's Life

THE WINDERMERE CUP

1999 poster

THE SAME morning that her Australian countrymen were upset by the Husky crew, the Windermere Cup changed Jenni Hogan's life, her home, her career, and even her name.

That's because while eighteen-year-old Jenni Vesnaver was rowing for Australia's Olympic crew team at the 1997 Cup, she accepted an unexpected scholarship offer from UW.

"Yes, the Windermere Cup, to me, is why I am in America," said the native of Adelaide, Australia. As a Huskies' captain and a two-time national champion, Hogan was one of a small few to have competed in five Windermere Cups (four with UW, one with Australia's national team) in the event's first quarter-century.

Her UW career ended in 2002, but she stayed in Seattle following graduation, becoming a popular TV personality in Western Washington. For her reporting job she rose around 3 a.m. each day to tell commuters at 4:30 how bad

Interstate 5 was to drive. In 2010, *Broadcast and Cable* magazine named her America's most-followed local TV anchor on Twitter. A year later she was a finalist for a national Shorty award, the "Oscars of Twitter."

While Hogan and her husband, Josh Hogan, were raising a toddler, she became a co-founder and chief strategy officer at Tagboard, a technology company that collects live postings of social media by hashtags for display. She also founded the Go Girl Academy, a career-acceleration program for women, and started Mission Hot Mama, a blog to inspire mothers to "release their inner hotness and shine."

In 2011 this dynamo stood among screaming fans at the Montlake Cut for the 25th Windermere Cup, when her Huskies hosted world-rowing power Cambridge University from England, as well as Stanford and Oklahoma. Only now she worked as the color analyst for ROOT Sports' live broadcast of that year's race—the same race in which she defeated national teams from Great Britain, Romania, and Egypt, among others.

She still loves the Windermere Cup.

"I've never seen anything like it. It's amazing," Hogan said, speaking from the lobby of the Maxwell Hotel in Seattle's lower Queen Anne neighborhood, a few blocks from her old job as traffic anchor for KIRO 7 TV. "Just going through the Cut, the audience can actually influence the race. Their screaming and cheering energizes the athletes, so in the final 500 meters, where you can win or lose the race and your body is telling you to stop, you now have these other people who can get in your head and tell you to keep going."

MEASURING UP WHILE DOWN UNDER

Hogan's story about how she began rowing is as unique as the race she loved.

Hogan, then Jenni Vesnaver, grew up playing basketball. She was the second child of father Livio Vesnaver, who immigrated by boat to Australia from Italy when he was eight, and Lisa, a financial analyst for the Australian government. They lived in the coastal town of Adelaide, the "wine capital" of Southern Australia, where Livio worked as a bank teller until the technology boom swept through their country and he got laid off. Jenni was only a teenager then.

When she was fourteen, Australia was selected to host the 2000 Summer Olympics. With six years to prepare, the government identified top athletes from Australia's high schools and brought them to select national sports institutes, which then ran tests to place the candidates in sports that leaders like John Boultbee, eventual director of the Australian Institute of Sport, felt offered the best opportunity for that candidate to produce a gold medal.

Boultbee brought Australia's national Olympic crews to the 1997 Windermere Cup.

"My sport was rowing, [based] purely on my body. My arm span is twelve centimeters longer than my height," said Hogan, who is over six feet tall. "Apparently I have good leverage," she said, pantomiming a rowing stroke. "But I remember going down to a lake with my parents for the first time and saying, 'I'm not going to fit in that because it's too skinny and small. I'm going to fall out.'"

The South Australia Sports Institute was no country club.

The 2015 Huskies women carry their shell back to Conibear Shellhouse after winning first place in the Windermere Cup.

Hogan was attached to heart monitors, breathing devices, and various machines to measure stamina, fitness, and conditioning in an effort to maximize her—and ultimately Australia's—performance for the Olympics. The program was modeled after East Germany's legendary and intense athletic training.

The program worked. At the time, Australia had the world's fifty-third most populous country, with fewer people than lived in Texas. Yet Aussies won the fourth-most medals at the Sydney Games. Australia's medal count (fifty-eight) was only one fewer than China, the world's most populous country, with over 1.2 billion citizens at that time.

The program worked for rowing and for Hogan.

By 1996 Hogan and her pairs crew partner, Melissa Nyveld, were considered Australia's shoo-ins to win the world championships. They had competed together there the previous year, and Hogan was in peak condition.

"The only thing we had to do was win our national championship race and we would go to the world championships," Hogan explained.

SURVIVING ADVERSITY AT A CRITICAL MOMENT

But at the start of the 1996 Australian national championships, Nyveld's knee gave out.

"So I was faced with being the fittest I've ever been in my life and not being able to go to the world championships," Hogan said. "I watched the rest of these rowers go to the junior world championships, while I was left at home... That was a hard time in my career."

So Hogan quit rowing and transferred to beach volleyball at the sports institute.

Three months into her new stint, Australia's Olympic crew team called. They needed to replace a retiring member and round out their roster for the 1997 Windermere Cup. "All the junior girls had gone to the world championships except me," Hogan said. "So I got a phone call to join the big leagues, to go to the Windermere Cup and join the

Jenni Hogan earned a reputation as a champion rower in the UW rowing program, and after college she became a popular local TV personality.

Olympic boat that was going."

Come Windermere Cup 1997 in Seattle, Hogan was standing on the metal grating atop the Montlake Bridge, watching opposing boats training under her. "When I thought the worst thing was happening in my career, it actually opened the door to something better. That's the lesson I tell people if something really bad happens. If that [injury] didn't happen to Melissa—poor Melissa—I wouldn't be over here. I wouldn't have been on the national eight team."

That bridge is where Eleanor McElvaine, coach for the Huskies' women's crew at the time, offered Hogan a scholarship.

A coach of a US university rowing power would offer a scholarship, on the spot, to a teenager from halfway around the world, one the coach had never seen compete?

"Well...I mean, I was on an Olympic eight, this top team, and I was just an eighteen-year-old," she said, trying not to brag. "So that was my recruiting trip, without me knowing it," she added, laughing.

Hogan wasn't totally alone in Seattle. Her uncle, Tom Eckmann, and aunt, Suzanne Keel-Eckmann, lived there. In fact, Jenni met them for the first time on that Windermere Cup trip. When she told them UW had offered her a scholarship and that she was inclined to say no, they responded, "If a school as good as U-Dub offers you a scholarship, you'd better take it."

"College rowing in Australia is not at the highest level," said Hogan. "Then I came here and saw how serious U-Dub was about rowing. I mean, everyone on my team was international caliber."

EXCEEDING EXPECTATIONS

Accepting UW's scholarship offer didn't mean she was in. Not yet.

First, she rented a movie. "I watched *Revenge of the Nerds* to learn what college life would be life in America." Then there were the entry requirements into UW. "I'd never heard of an SAT score. We don't do SATs in

> ❝Just going through the [Montlake] Cut, the audience can actually influence the race. Their screaming and cheering energizes the athletes, so in the final, where you can win or lose the race and your body is telling you to stop, you now have these other people who can get in your head and tell you to keep going. ❞

JENNI HOGAN

Australia." To complete the Scholastic Assessment Test, she took a three-hour flight to Sydney, the only SAT examination center in her country, and took the test with a handful of other countrymen trying to get into US colleges. No SAT prep course; no studying. She just went and took the test cold, her athletic and academic careers on the line.

"Growing up, instead of coloring books on the coffee table, my dad had IQ books for some reason, Hogan said. So this SAT stuff was very similar to those IQ books that my dad had planted."

The night before Thanksgiving in the US, she received her two SAT scores. She saw her individual score in the math section and the one in reading—and was crushed. Each score was way below what she needed to get into Washington, yet she was only weeks away from flying to Seattle.

She didn't understand the two individual scores added together provided her official SAT score.

"We don't have Thanksgiving in Australia," she said, "so I didn't know why no one from the States was calling me back for four days."

The following Monday, Huskies' coaches were laughing at Hogan. She had an excellent total score, easily enabling her to enroll at UW.

Hogan came to UW thinking she would stay a year and return home. Then she learned getting a degree wouldn't be such a grind, since the academics and athletic programs worked in harmony at Washington.

"The difference was athletics and education worked hand-in-hand here. In Australia, they were competing against each other," she said. "Trying to get a degree in Australia while competing...it probably would've taken me six or eight years, because I had to train three times a day and then go to school part-time. Here, it was awesome. You could work out and work with the academic side and actually graduate at the same time."

In fact, she graduated in three and a half years with a double major: economics and communications.

But she didn't just study. Hogan won four Pac-10 titles in her four rowing seasons at UW. Her second of two national titles came in 2002 when she served as team captain and stroke on the Huskies' junior-varsity eight.

Moments after that race, Hogan walked away from the sport.

"It had been ten years of rowing, so I retired," recalled Hogan. "I've been asked so many times to join the alumni rowing, the masters rowing. It sounds so odd to say that, but there is no way. I can't casually row. Since day one, when they identified me for rowing, it's been all about winning."

Nyveld, her former rowing partner whose knee injury changed the course of Hogan's life, remained "like a sister" to Hogan. "I've called Melissa many times and thanked her for hurting her knee," Hogan said, laughing. Hogan stayed with Nyveld in 2009 when she visited Australia.

"That one phone call to come to the Windermere Cup changed my life. What I thought was the worst moment of my life...turned into something that has made my life so great." ∎

The men and women of Washington's 2015 rowing program, including the women's eight crew who clinched a nine-year winning streak in that year's Windermere Cup.

A unique aerial perspective of rowers racing through the narrow man-made channel, which is called the Montlake Cut, connecting Portage Bay and Lake Washington.

The Romanians Come to Stay

SANDA (HANGAN) MITCHELL was at the center of the most controversial event in the history of the Windermere Cup.

It cost her national coach his job. But it also spawned new, better lives for six women from Eastern Europe who came to the 2001 Windermere Cup, then never returned home.

Mitchell's trek to the Windermere Cup started in the 1990s, over 5,000 miles from Seattle and the Montlake Cut. She was then Sanda Hangan, the second-oldest of four children (older sister Laura, younger sister Daniela, and younger brother Ovidiu) raised by Elena and Alexandru Hangan in Lozna, Romania, a farming village near Romania's northern border with what is now Ukraine.

When not home raising the children, Elena put her accounting skills to work in the flower-shop business she and her husband ran, while Alexandru also worked at

2001 poster

a glass factory.

The family lived in a countryside house with no running water and no bathroom. It was not till 2010, the year Sanda Hangan became Sanda Mitchell by marriage, that she built a bathroom with running water for her parents in their Lozna home.

Yet Mitchell (née Hangan) considers herself w1990s Romania.

"With my family's flower shop, we were pretty well off," Mitchell said. "With dad's job at the glass factory, too, we had a pretty good life. I feel we really didn't have a hard life, like a lot of people there did."

When Mitchell was just beginning grade school, the Soviet Union collapsed. Social programs and basic, everyday necessities dried up in Romania, Bulgaria, and neighboring Balkan countries. Potable water and electricity were limited and, in some places, nonexistent. Romania was then sixteen years away from joining the European Union.

The Hangan family had a television, something not all Romanians owned. Mitchell remembers being six years old watching a Romanian-dubbed version of *Dallas*, the American TV drama that depicted rich, feuding Texas-oil families and was a pop-culture hit worldwide during its run from 1978-91.

"My sister and I loved *Dallas*," she said. "We pretended to speak English like they did. We loved their lifestyle. I didn't think life could be like that."

When she was fourteen, Mitchell took up rowing and immediately showed remarkable aptitude. The national rowing program invited her to its training center in Orsova, where she'd live and go to school full time. That was on the border with Serbia in southwest Romania, a ten-hour train ride from home.

Training ran eleven and a half months of the year. During the academic year, they had an early morning practice, then classes, lunch, and a grueling afternoon back on the water.

"That's how they do rowing there," she said, explaining how Romania clung to the Soviet-era style of developing powerful teams for international athletic competitions, where they could gain prestige.

"I had it better than most. We had food. We had nice warm beds and everything. In the rest of the country, there were shortages. People didn't have money. They still don't. We were really sheltered from the real Romanian world."

That shelter came at a price.

While finishing second in the world championships in 1998 and first in '99, Mitchell and her national teammates had three practices per day.

Two years into her national team training program, Poland's men's and women's national teams backed out of the 2001 Windermere Cup.

Mitchell had no way of knowing how that development half a world away would change her life.

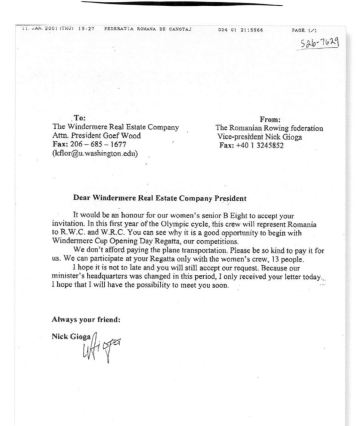

The Romanian Rowing Federation writes to accept the invitation from Windermere Real Estate's president, Geoff (misspelled in the letter) Wood, to send only their women's crew to the 2001 Windermere Cup.

CHANGING TEAMS LAST MINUTE

The Polish actually had backed out the Cup twice. First in 2000, the year Egypt became the second crew from Africa to compete in the regatta (South Africa was the first, in 1995).

Kajetan Broniewski, then executive director of the Polish Rowing Federation, sent a fax to the University of Washington in mid-April of 2000, just weeks before the regatta, saying, in part, "We are sorry for all the trouble."

The following November, UW's senior associate athletic director Gary Barta and Windermere Real Estate president Geoff Wood sent Broniewski another formal invitation, this time to the 2001 Windermere Cup. The letter stated:

In exchange for your teams' participation, Windermere Real Estate will underwrite the following expenses for one men's and women's international rowing team: round-trip airfare to/from Seattle for thirteen (13) team members for both men's and women's teams, including ten (10) rowers, plus one (1) coxswain and two (2) coaches/team leaders per team, for a total of 26 people." The letter went on to offer meals and lodging for the 26-member travel party, ground transportation to and from scheduled events, access to two "high-quality racing shells and a coaching launch," plus "gifts, social activities, and area tours.

The invitation also outlined a schedule of activities which included a press conference the day after the teams' arrival, a sponsor/athletes' dinner on Thursday, public appearances at a Seattle-area hospital and/or school on Friday, race-day events on Saturday and departure on Sunday. That was the standard Windermere Cup invitation.

"Please note your organization is responsible for bringing your own oars," the letter added.

Weeks later, the Polish backed out again. (The men's national team finally made it to the Windermere Cup in 2003).

By the time Poland dropped out, Bob Ernst knew which teams he wanted as replacements: Croatia's first-time Olympic bronze-winning crew of twenty- and thirty-something men, and Romania's national women's crew for the women's race.

"I particularly wanted [Romania] to come because they were the world champions," Ernst said of Hangan and her teammates, who had won gold at the 1999 and 2000 World Junior Championships. The Romanians had won gold in the women's eight for the previous two Olympics (1996 and 2000).

By then, however, it was early 2001, the off season for

Romania's 2001 national women's crew and entourage stand behind UW's famed rowing coach Dick Erickson aboard Scott Hannah's yacht, the *Eleuthera*, shortly before the women disembarked the ship and disappeared.

Hangan and her teammates. The rowers were off their peak shapes and strokes.

Late that January, with less than four months before race day, Romanian Rowing Federation vice president Nick Gioga replied via fax to UW and Wood, "It would be an honour for our women's senior B Eight to accept your invitation" to the 2001 Windermere Cup. "I hope it is not to (sic) late and you will still accept our request. Because our minister's headquarters was changed in this period, I only received your letter today."

Gioga would be the coach leading the national women's team of thirteen to Seattle. "We don't afford paying the plane transportation," he explained in his second language of English. "Please be so kind to pay for it for us." He didn't know that Windermere pays travel expenses for visiting Cup teams.

Mitchell packed her training gear and only a few days' worth of clothes and supplies. When she left Orsova to take the long journey to Seattle that last day of April 2001, it was just another far-flung trip to yet another rowing competition to her and her family. No big goodbyes.

"I was entering college there. I was in the top five on the national team. My goal was the Olympics, and I had a great chance to be on Romania's Olympics team," she said. "It wasn't like I was planning on escaping."

MEETING HER COMPETITION

Despite Poland backing out, the UW and Windermere saw the 2001 Windermere Cup as the best, deepest field yet assembled in the fifteen years of the event.

The women's team from University of Victoria, British Columbia, Canada, was also invited to compete that year. Its presence provided a rematch of the history-making 2000 Henley Royal Regatta outside London, when Washington's

women's varsity eight defeated Victoria to win the grand finale, the Henley Prize, the first year the famed British regatta presented a trophy for the women's eight.

UW women's crew coach Jan Harville said on the eve of the 15th Windermere Cup, "It's really going to be spectacular."

"This is a statement on behalf of the University of Washington, Windermere, and the Seattle Yacht Club that we want to bring the best competition in the world to Seattle," Ernst said in the February 23, 2001, edition of the *Seattle Times*.

Hangan and her dozen Romanian teammates boarded KLM Flight 1358 out of Bucharest and, after a stop in Amsterdam, they arrived in Seattle on a Monday evening. Ernst's truck and two UW rental vans met the Romanians at SeaTac Airport and drove them to the Silver Cloud Inn north of UW, their home for the week. They had dinner at the hotel that night and the next morning, May 1 (Ziua muncii, Labor Day in Romania, a national public holiday to honor its workers), the Croatian men and the Romanian women ate breakfast at the Husky Union Building (the HUB) on campus.

The teams held a press conference at UW's shell house, enjoyed an afternoon bus tour of Seattle, practiced on the water, then ate dinner in a UW dormitory. The next day the teams attended a small reception at the UW shellhouse and then a larger, formal dinner event at the Columbia Tower Club on the seventy-sixth floor of Seattle's tallest building.

Hangan and her Romanian teammates were awed by far more than the sweeping views atop the second-tallest building on the West Coast. They were awed by Seattle's lush spring blooms. By the food. The houses. The hospitality. The Friday visit to Seattle Children's Hospital.

By everything in America.

"I couldn't believe how clean it was. It was so clean. There were no holes in the pavement!" Hangan said a dozen years later. "There was no trash lying around. And the breakfasts in the hotel! I remember I didn't know how to use the waffle iron. And the pancakes, all the pastries. I kept thinking, 'This is wonderful!'" Even the dinners in the dorm wowed the Romanians. "I remember all this food we had!" Hangan said. "It was a completely different world."

Intensity, power, and focus are a must to compete in the Windermere Cup, and here the women's eight crews make it look easy.

"The girls from the Washington boat were so nice. They were always talking with us and smiling that whole week. It was a really great environment; nothing I had ever experienced."

During one of her workouts on Union Bay, Mitchell struck up a conversation about crew with then UW senior Nicole Rogers, who rowed bow seat on the Huskies' women's varsity eight crew, the nine-time defending Pac-10-champion and two-time Windermere Cup champion team. "I remember being in the shell house and her telling us they only have one practice per day plus a separate individual workout," Mitchell recalled. "I said, 'What?! One practice a day!' It was like a dream come true. We had three practices a day, and some of those were three- or four-hour practices."

Mitchell and her teammates were experiencing what their contemporaries back home thought was only a dream.

ROLLING BACK THE CLOCK

Late in 1999, a documentary film crew from the Graduate School of Journalism at University of California, Berkeley, visited Bulgaria, Romania's Balkan neighbor to the south. The young American students were filming a production about Bulgaria's future after the Soviet Union collapse, when the Kremlin no longer supported its former satellite states in Eastern Europe.

One snowy December night, the Berkeley crew filmed students from the national university in Sofia dancing in a dance club on campus. The students drank water or maybe Coca-Colas all night. The bottled beers stocked in the cooler behind the bar remained mostly untouched, since the students couldn't afford much more than water. In a dark corner of the club, the Americans interviewed the Bulgarian students, asking each what they wished they possessed more than anything in the world.

Shouting over the techno-bass music thumping through the dark club, the majority of the students answered, "A US passport."

While Romania was somewhat better off and more progressive in its post-Soviet existence than Bulgaria, that rose-colored prism through which the Bulgarian students viewed America was shared by Hangan and her teammates.

By race day, after a week of relative decadence, some of

Mitchell's teammates considered the possibility of staying in Seattle, of not getting on the plane home, back to the spartan, relatively impoverished living in Eastern Europe.

"I knew other girls wanted to stay, to not go home," Mitchell said. "But not me."

After a race-day breakfast in the Don James Center inside Husky Stadium, the Romanians climbed into their borrowed shell and, at 11:20 a.m., broke away from Washington's boat at the starting line.

Theirs was the sixteenth of seventeen races slated for the 2001 Windermere Cup.

The crews rowed between the log booms that stretched from Union Bay to Montlake Cut, which were jammed with boats and screaming fans.

The Romanian women took an early lead in the open waters of Union Bay. But once they neared the unfamiliar Cut, the Romanians had no answer for their UW hosts, nor for the roaring crowds that spurred the Huskies' push.

"We were coming off our off-water season," explained Mitchell. "We were not yet totally adjusted like U-Dub was. We weren't ready for the pace, for this level of racing. Not yet."

The Huskies ultimately swamped their visitors.

Gioga, the coach who came all the way to Seattle thinking this would be a good tune-up race for his world-class Romanian women's eight, was furious.

"We lost the race," Mitchell said. "It was not looking good for us. The coaches were mad. We knew we were going back to get yelled at and to work really hard, which was not fair."

Suddenly, in the gloom of humiliating defeat and anticipating what awaited them in training upon returning home, Mitchell changed her mind. And her life.

CHANGING DIRECTIONS

Hours after the race, the Romanians sat aboard the wood-adorned *Eleuthera*, a yacht owned by Scott Hannah, the chief executive officer of Pacific Valley Foods of Bellevue, Washington. Hannah brought his boat to the Windermere Cup every year.

His boat was no dinghy. It's a sixty-one-foot Hatteras motor yacht with a salon deck and three bedrooms down below. "The girls had been telling their coach, which he relayed to

me, that our boat was bigger than their apartments back in Bucharest," Hannah said.

"Those girls were overwhelmed by all the boats and the scene."

For years after, in the cabin of his boat, Hannah kept a photograph from that night of the Romanian women gathered in the main salon of his boat with Washington's iconic crew coach, Dick Erickson, leaning his arm on a table in front of the Romanians, wearing a navy-blue rain jacket. One of the Romanian coaches sits immediately behind Erickson, dressed in a blue suit coat, blue shirt and bright gold tie. On his head rests a Soviet Navy officer's service cap, which

Crews row back to Conibear Shellhouse after participating in the Opening Day crew races.

Hannah had acquired from St. Petersburg in the former Soviet Union.

That photo was taken only two months before Erickson passed away suddenly at his home in Marysville, Washington, at the age of sixty-five. The picture was also the last time the Romanian coaches saw half their team.

Mitchell had joined six teammates in their idea to stay in Seattle, to not board the next day's noon bus from their hotel to SeaTac Airport for the Sunday flight back to Bucharest.

When Hannah docked at the Conibear Shellhouse, Mitchell and five teammates (bow and two-time world-champion Alina Tabacaru, four seat Monica Diaconu, six seat Oana Soptea, two seat Anda Stefanescu, and reserve Mihaela Halip) disembarked the boat but never made it back to the hotel.

Hannah had left the Romanian women, who were unattended by their coaches, on the dock, expecting them to board a bus assigned to return them to the Silver Cloud Inn. It might've been 200 yards from the dock to the shell house parking lot.

"They disappeared," Ernst said. "Some of them got connected with Romanian people who lived in the Seattle area and just hid out. And the coach was pissed. Here his job was simply to come over here and make this race, and when they get to the airport on Sunday, three or four of the girls were MIA. Nobody knew where they were—supposedly didn't know where they were. It was a big hoo-haw."

STARTING ANEW ABROAD

Turned out, the Romanian women had already lined up homes where they could stay with host families in the Seattle area, Mitchell recalled. Those host families' connections came through a man named Danut Moraru.

Moraru attended high school in Husi, Romania, then studied computer science at the University of Iasi in the Romanian city of Iasi. He left teaching and moved to the United States in 1996 to work for Microsoft in the Seattle suburb of Redmond. He was well-networked among Romanians throughout the Pacific Northwest, and he worked that Windermere Cup week in May 2001 as translator for the delegation visiting from his home country.

Mitchell said Moraru had arranged for the six Romanians to stay in three Seattle-area homes. Moraru and the rowers talked among themselves during the postrace social time, deciding who would go to which of his friends' houses. Because Hangan had only met Moraru, not his friends, she insisted on staying at his house across Lake Washington. "He said, 'Okay,'" Hangan added.

So while Hannah and Erickson were trying to socialize with the Romanians aboard the *Eleuthera,* six of the women were planning a life-altering decision, one that would have repercussions for their families, friends, and two coaches.

"Yeah, it was pretty selfish. But I was twenty years old," Mitchell said years later. "I didn't have a lot of time to think

about it. If I'd had the time and thought about it more, I might have gone back home." Instead, "we all got into [Moraru's] car."

Mischelle Day, who served as the lead hostess and social-events organizer for visiting teams at nearly every Windermere Cup, was one of the first to realize half of Romania's team was missing. The Romanians' flight from SeaTac Airport to Amsterdam was departing at 1:50 p.m. the next day.

She immediately called Erickson, who called Ernst, who got the University of Washington and Seattle police departments involved. But the extra hours of fruitless searches and phone calls only heightened what was, for the Cup's organizers, an international crisis.

"For me, it was the worst boating Opening Day and Windermere Cup imaginable," Day said years later.

"The coach—he was a very successful coach in Romania—he lost his job over it," said Ernst, who was essentially the Romanians', and especially Gioga's, rowing host.

Ernst called the situation "a train wreck" and explained, "Oh, it was huge in the press. You see, after the fall of the Soviet (Eastern) Bloc, there was no such thing supposedly as political asylum anymore. Supposedly, because these guys are all our buddies now. I mean, they aren't Communists anymore; they are just Romanians. That made it really complicated for these people who wanted to stay behind. And, of course, their country wanted them back and their rowing federation wanted them back and their coach wanted them back. And they weren't about to go."

RETURNING TO HER MISSION

As Moraru secluded the Romanians from the Seattle authorities' search, he phoned Mitchell's by-now terrified parents back in Lozna. "You have my word," Moraru told Mr. and Mrs. Hangan, "she will finish college."

And she did.

More than a chance to live in the United States, more than merely rowing, above all, Mitchell wanted to get a college degree.

And because she'd met UW's rowers, hung out with them all week and seen firsthand how good UW's rowing program was, she wanted to go to the University of Washington.

Washington's opponents cried foul, accusing the Huskies of using the Windermere Cup essentially as a recruiting tool for international rowers.

"I don't even remember all the permutations that got them from staying behind to [entering] UW," said Jan Harville, the Washington women's crew coach who recruited Mitchell and Tabacaru. "Of course, we couldn't put them up. That's an NCAA rules violation. They were taken in by families. And they were nannies and housekeepers and all that kind of stuff, until they got student visas to go to school."

Mitchell and Tabacaru, who was from Bacau, Romania, had an advantage over their teammates who also stayed behind in Seattle. They spoke English the best, which enabled them to easily pass the TOEFL (Test of English as a Foreign Language), which foreigners were required to pass to enter American universities. While Mitchell and Tabacaru were accepted into the University of Washington, the four other Romanians who couldn't pass the TOEFL tried blending into American society outside of college.

As a freshman, Mitchell was named the Pac-10 women's crew newcomer of the year. She rowed as UW's four seat in the junior-varsity eight that won the JV gold medal at the 2002 NCAA Championships, and she was the stroke on the JV eight that finished second in the 2003 NCAA finals, where UW finished third as a team. In 2004 the Huskies promoted her to stroke on the varsity eight for her junior season, and she became an All-American. In 2005 she and the Huskies won the nineteenth Windermere Cup and the petite final at the NCAA championships.

MAKING HER BIGGEST DECISION YET

During college Sanda Hangan found a job at the new Acme Bowl bowling alley and night spot near Southcenter Mall, south of Seattle. There she met James Mitchell, who was working in mobile-device advertising in Seattle. The chance meeting would prove to be her best move as a Husky.

> **66** My goal was the Olympics, and I had a great chance to be on Romania's Olympics team. It wasn't like I was planning on escaping. **99**
>
> SANDA MITCHELL

"When I worked there, I got hit on a lot. Every day I got hit on," she said, comparing Acme's customers to James Mitchell. "He had a friend who was a bartender, and he told his friend that he was interested in me. I said, 'No way. He doesn't even talk to me!'"

Then, during her senior season, she herniated a disk in her back—brutal pain for a rower.

For the 20th Windermere Cup in 2006, Washington's women hosted the Czechoslovakian national team, which beat the UW varsity eight by 1.27 seconds in the women's final. Her Husky career and senior season ended later that spring with a disappointing sixth-place finish, with Sanda Hangan ailing and in the six seat for the varsity eight petite final on Lake Natomas outside Sacramento, California.

The next month she fulfilled Moraru's promise on his long-distance phone call to her parents in Romania: she graduated from UW. She had an interest in early childhood teaching. She'd also developed another interest. By graduation, James Mitchell had more than grown on her from their time spent at Acme Bowl. "All these guys would talk to me there and they were pushy and loud. He was not pushy," she said. "He was very, very respectful. From the first week he finally talked to me, I could tell he was a unique person. Very smart, and very, very respectful of women. I had never met a man like that. Three years later we got married."

That was 2010. Mitchell hadn't rowed since that herniated disk limited her as a UW senior. "I can't even get on an erg machine without it bothering me," she said years later. "I do some jogging, some hot yoga, some physical therapy."

While her former crewmate Tabacaru found a home in Edmonds, a suburb north of Seattle, Mitchell became a head preschool teacher on Mercer Island. When she and James had their first child, son Preston, a few years later, Mitchell became a full-time mom. Still, she wanted to return to school for a master's degree in education and become a teacher.

She became comfortable in her American life, and for that she has the Windermere Cup to thank. ■

Fighting for an early lead in the field is key to out-rowing your competitors. Here the UW men's rowers are earning their champion reputation.

Windermere Cup's Best Resource: the Rowers

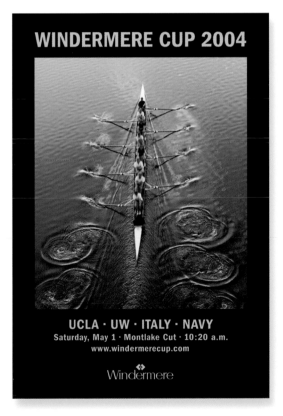

WINDERMERE CUP 2004

UCLA · UW · ITALY · NAVY
Saturday, May 1 · Montlake Cut · 10:20 a.m.
www.windermerecup.com

Windermere

2004 poster

NOT ONLY is the Windermere Cup a top-flight event with some of the world's best crew teams, the rowers themselves aren't exactly shabby, either.

Sixteen members of the national championship crew team made the 2011 Pac-10 All-Academic team.

The list of majors among crew that year was typical and looked more like a Rhodes Scholar competition: biochemistry, mathematics, physics, pre-engineering, and anthropology, among others.

Take a single quarter in the 2010 academic year at UW.

The Huskies' thirty-nine rowers combined for a grade-point average of 3.30 that term, second among men's sports only to the Huskies' men's tennis at 3.48, a team that had one-third the number of athletes.

REVISITING THE CUP YEARS LATER

Like Australia's Jenni Hogan, Roberto Blanda competed for his home country against Washington at his first Windermere Cup.

That was in 1989, when Italy's men's eight beat UW and New Zealand to win the third Cup. Like Hogan, Blanda says the Windermere Cup changed his life.

Former Huskies Director of Rowing Bob Ernst recruited Blanda to row for Washington from 1993 to '95, when the Windermere Cup was attracting crews from across the world.

Blanda won all three Windermere Cups when he was at UW: over Dartmouth College and Humboldt of Germany in '93; The Netherlands and Stanford in '94; and South Africa in 1995.

He also continued Husky crew's excellence off the water. He graduated cum laude from UW in 1995 with a Bachelor of Arts degree in linguistics, focusing on French and the Romance languages. He was then accepted into graduate school at England's Oxford University, where he continued rowing, beating Cambridge on the River Thames in "The Boat Race," all while getting a master's in educational research methodology.

Blanda went on to become the general manager of human relations for Toyota Motor Italia; the corporate human resources and organization director for Mercedes Benz Italia; the sales and marketing manager for Mercedes Benz's financial services in Italy; and then the head of HR and general services for British American Tobacco Italy.

Ernst contacted Blanda for the 2004 Windermere Cup to enlist his help in getting the Italian national team back to the Montlake Cut.

That Cup had Blanda, by then an executive in his thirties, acting as head of the delegation for his home country.

"It is really special for me to be back here, because my experience here changed my life," Blanda told the UW *Daily* newspaper in 2004. "I have raced in different races worldwide, and the Windermere Cup is a special and unique race."

ROWING IN A WAR ZONE

Ante Kusurin grew up in Zagreb, Croatia. Like many rowers, he took up the sport of crew relatively late, as a teenager.

Yet within a couple years, he became a two-time junior world champion.

He was also an A student and was looking for colleges to attend come 2001, the same year Ernst had invited Croatia's senior national team to row in the Windermere Cup. "All of them talked about this kid," Ernst told the *Seattle Post-Intelligencer* in 2006. "'We know this one guy who should come here...'"

Thanks to that tip at the Windermere Cup, Ernst aggressively recruited Kusurin. The only American universities the Croatian had heard of were Harvard and Princeton, Ivy League rowing powers.

But he chose Washington, he said, because he'd learned quickly that he would be tested most at UW.

"It's the toughest [rowing] program in the USA and the world," Kusurin said. "And, I like evergreens."

The Huskies also had several Serbians in its rowing program, a tricky and bothersome fact for Kusurin, who was

No pain, no gain, as they say, and both UW men's and women's crews know that motto, competing with each other even in their daily workouts.

Photo: Scott Eklund/Red Box Pictures

only two years removed from watching Croatia and Serbia wage war against each other.

"The war had just ended and there was still a lot of frustration," Kusurin told the *Post-Intelligencer* in 2006 about his freshman year at Washington. "I met the two Serbian guys and it became obvious to me: I don't think we should mix sports and politics."

His freshman-year adjustment wasn't too disruptive. Kusurin was the six seat on the freshman eight that won a gold medal and Stewards Cup at the IRA national finals.

In fact, the Croatian eventually became roommates with two Serbians, unheard of back home in the volatile Balkans. Kusurin and Belgrade-native Aljosa Corovic shared a house in Seattle with Corovic's fellow Serb Alex Slovic, a UW tennis player.

As a sophomore in 2003, Kusurin earned a silver medal on the varsity eight at the IRAs.

He spent a redshirt year in 2004 back home, training with the Croatian National Team, but a conflict with his coaches left him off Croatia's Olympic team that year.

He returned to Seattle in 2005, again wowed by the spectacle of the Windermere Cup, which by then was in its eighteenth year. "It's like an all-star game. It's not a championship game,

> " It is really special for me to be back here, because my experience here changed my life. I have raced in different races worldwide, and the Windermere Cup is a special and unique race. "
>
> ROBERTO BLANDO

2012 brought the University of Virginia men's team to compete with the UW's and Argentina's men's teams.

but I've been to six world championships, and nowhere did I see anything like this with all the people," Kusurin told the *P-I* in 2006. "It's a one-of-a-kind event. It makes you a star for a day."

Kusurin rowed four years at UW, winning three Windermere Cups (when he was a redshirt senior in 2006, the Huskies lost to the Russian Rowing Federation). After graduating from Washington as its rowing captain in 2006, Kusurin fulfilled his dream of attending graduate school at the University of Oxford's Saïd Business School.

He competed in doubles sculls at the 2008 Beijing Olympics while a rower on Croatia's national team, where he remained for more than eight years.

He eventually became a financial analyst in London, then an associate at One Equity Partners, a venture-capital and private-equity firm in New York. "He works for a Wall Street company that takes over international companies," is how Ernst put it in 2013.

ROLLING UP HIS SLEEVES

Kusurin was also involved in one of the more unusual Windermere Cups in the event's history.

American twins Cameron and Tyler Winklevoss gained fame for suing Facebook founder Mark Zuckerberg in 2004, claiming he stole their networking idea,

MICHAEL CALLAHAN

The Latest Leader of UW's Rowing Dynasty

Michael Callahan was born in Honolulu and grew up in six states, moving with his family to follow his father's career as a submarine captain in the US Navy. So boats and water have always been integral to the coach of Washington's men's rowing dynasty.

Callahan was coach Bob Ernst's captain on the 1996 Washington Huskies' crew team. He won gold medals at the world junior and under twenty-three championships in that decade. And he accepted Ernst's offer to be coaching intern at Washington in 2001.

After the 2004 Athens Olympics—Callahan was a spare on the US team at those Games—Ernst convinced Callahan to move back across the country to Seattle to become Washington's freshman rowing coach.

In 2007 Ernst decided to be UW's women's coach again. He made Callahan, then only thirty-four, his successor as men's coach.

That worked out okay. The Huskies entered the 30th Windermere Cup in 2016 having won an unprecedented five consecutive Intercollegiate Rowing Association national championships under Callahan.

How does he find the men who build a dynasty? When recruiting, Callahan seeks to get inside a teenager's psyche to find out if he has the makeup to survive Washington's training, let alone compete for the Huskies'.

Some of the young men he evaluates may have picked up an oar just days ago.

Callahan spends some of his summers across the globe, recruiting in Europe and beyond. His Huskies' roster for 2016 included rowers from Switzerland, England, Slovenia, Australia, Italy, Serbia, Croatia, and Germany.

The result is a team that is one of the most diverse and accomplished in the country, and not just on the water.

"I really enjoy the fact that at the University of Washington we can go get the best rower in his age in the world. We are that attractive to him," the coach said. "It's interesting, they are attracted not only by the rowing, but the school, too. They say, `I really like your computer engineering program. I really like your mathematics program.'"

A snapshot of the 2011 team, for instance, showed in one academic term thirty-nine Washington rowers combined for a grade-point average of 3.30. That was second among men's sports only to the 3.48 of Huskies men's tennis, which has one-third the number of athletes on its team.

"It goes back to our founding principles that we have here, that everyone here is performing to their potential level," Callahan said. "It's become the ethos to what we do here."

Callahan coaches with competition as his central theme—in everything.

Walk through the weight room in Graves Annex and you'll see the accent isn't on raw strength. It's on speed and endurance, just like out on the water.

The coach Ernst calls "a great manager" is also part businessman, perhaps more than any coach on UW's campus.

Sure, college coaches in all sports work year round. But how many win multiple national championships while also managing the challenges associated with rowing, a sport often underfunded at the collegiate level?

"You have to become a fundraiser, a PR-marketing-brand guy. You have to figure out a lot of skill sets," said Callahan.

The glittering Conibear Shellhouse was renovated in 2005 at a cost of $18 million. The money came from donations by alumni and friends of UW and Huskies' rowing, including donations from Windermere.

By the time he'd led the Huskies to their fifth-consecutive national rowing championship, Callahan's leadership had indeed transcended sports. He was the only sports person named as one of *Seattle* Magazine's most influential people of 2015. ■

which they'd developed while undergraduate rowers at Harvard.

The Winklevoss twins became more famous in the 2010 film *The Social Network* that detailed Facebook's start, the same year they were supposed to race in the twenty-fourth Windermere Cup. By then they were attending Saïd Business School with Kusurin.

Ernst again had tapped into his international network of former Husky rowers to line up Oxford, securing Kusurin's help to get England's famed crew to its first Windermere Cup. In fact, Kusurin escorted the Oxford team to Seattle for the event that week in May 2010.

That was two years after the Winklevoss twins advanced to the Beijing Olympics in a pairs boat for the United States, so they were still in prime racing condition. But the "Winklevii," as the twins were known, did not make it from Oxford to Seattle. They stayed in England due to…a volcano.

Iceland's Eyjafjallajökull volcano, specifically. The caldera

erupted multiple times that spring, sending clouds of ash eastward to cover neighboring continents and close major European airports, and throw the 2010 Windermere Cup into prerace chaos.

"We were lucky we had a race," Ernst said, "because they didn't even bring the whole team from London to Seattle. They had to come from Africa and all over the world."

The fans lining the Montlake Cut didn't know that. They were too busy roaring for Washington's men's and women's teams, which were themselves roaring to victory over Oxford and Syracuse.

"Ante ended up having to row in the race," said Ernst, who estimated 40,000 people attended that year's race. "He was here as chief of the delegation, an honored position, and he'd rowed on the Olympic team two summers before. But, I mean, the summer before the 2010 Windermere Cup for him was a lot of banking and not training."

Kusurin's return to UW wasn't triumphant that year. But, thanks to a volcano, it was unique. "He ended up stroking the Oxford boat," Ernst added. "He took off his three-piece suit and went out and raced."

MAKING THEIR OWN WAY

On a perfectly sunny and warm May morning in 2013, Ryan Schroeder was the six seat on Washington's eight-man varsity crew that swamped Cornell by more than twelve seconds and Dartmouth by more than eighteen to win the twenty-seventh Windermere Cup.

Schroeder went on to win yet another national championship that June. He rowed from the five seat in the Americans' gold-medal-boat in 2012's World Rowing Under 23 Championships. The native of Thousand Oaks, California, was also on the Pac-12 All-Academic second team that year.

All while he earned his degree in aeronautical engineering.

"The kids on our team are competitors,"

The 2012 Windermere Cup brought women's crews from Gonzaga and Argentina, but the UW women's crew won the Cup.

Ernst said. "Not only do they compete on the water, they compete in the classroom.

"Across the country, I think in rowing programs academic achievement is important. And I think one of the reasons that it's important is that nobody is going to hand you a contract to play another sport when you're done with college. The apex of our game is making it to the Olympics. And win a medal at the Olympics, and usually what you end up with is that, plus a whole bunch of bills to pay," said Ernst.

Schroeder's teammate, Sam Ojserkis, was the coxswain who barked Washington to the IRA national title in course-record time in 2012. That year he also coxed the US men's eight to a gold medal at the Under 23 World Championships in Trakai, Lithuania.

While at UW, Ojserkis was a three-time member of Pac-12's All-Academic first team, and in 2012 was the Pac-12 scholar athlete of the year. After graduating, he accepted an admissions offer to do graduate school at Cambridge University, where he hosted the Huskies when they raced on the Thames in 2013.

Seamus Labrum turned down a chance to follow Ojserkis to England. Another member of that 2012 UW crew which won the Windermere Cup and the IRA national tile, Labrum was on the Pac-12's All-Academic first team with Ojserkis in 2012. Labrum was a double major at Washington, in communications and political science, and earned a spot on the dean's list in 2011 and 2012. Labrum was also accepted to Cambridge for graduate school, but instead chose to attend UW's School of Law.

Said Ernst, "It is pretty rewarding when you see the number of student athletes who actually get into med school, who get into law school, who get into the MBA programs that they want to get into. It's a big hallmark. It's a big part of Washington rowing.

"That's the difference. Our athletes understand that they have to make their own way when they graduate and after they finish their sport. For the most part, they take advantage of that opportunity." ■

The Argentinian
men's and
women's crews
proved not only
fine competitors,
but left behind a
reputation for
being a lot of fun.

Photo: Red Box
Pictures

How the Windermere Cup Helped Prepare UW Rowers for the Military

2012 poster

On a cool May morning in 2012, Rob Squires drove UW in the twenty-sixth Annual Windermere Cup to a whopping 14.8-second victory over Argentina's national team boat, plus Virginia and Oregon State.

The UW men and the women, themselves winners by 18 seconds over Gonzaga and 28 seconds over Argentina, had each won their sixth consecutive Windermere Cup.

By June, Squires was driving to a national title in course-record time as the stroke of Washington's varsity four crew. Squires and UW swamped archrival California and the rest of the field at the 110th Intercollegiate Rowing Association championships that year in Cherry Hill, New Jersey.

A few days later, Squires received his history degree from UW.

And less than a week after that, Ensign Robert Squires drove across country to report to a guided-missile destroyer and become a newly commissioned officer in the United States Navy. The *USS Michael Murphy*, christened in May that year, was in its final stages of construction in Bath, Maine.

Now that's a productive month and a half.

"It's pretty rewarding to reach this point. And it's just a beginning," Squires said before he left on his cross-country drive to his ship and new life. "It can even be more rewarding from here."

Squires was one of three seniors among that spring's rock-hard, national-champion Huskies' crew team that became officers in our nation's military. Reiner Hershaw, the two seat on the champion open four crew, was commissioned as a new second lieutenant in the US Marine Corps. So was teammate C.J. Miller.

Squires headed immediately into active duty, to a warship to fulfill the needs and missions of surface-warfare officers, the traditional backbone to the Navy. But Miller's and

For the 2012 Windermere Cup, UW hosted Argentina, Gonzaga, Virginia, and Oregon State.

Hershaw's military careers were delayed by the change in missions and reduction in US forces deployed to Iraq and Afghanistan into 2012. That draw-down caused a backlog in training assignments, so they didn't report to their first active-duty stations until the summer and fall, respectively, of 2013.

That didn't change their appreciation or perspective on the choices they'd made while at Washington and still in their early twenties, decisions that set them up for unique careers. "A lot of people will make a lot more money than me in other jobs. But it's about being able to serve," Hershaw said. "I've talked to a lot of guys, older guys whose chances have passed, who have really regretted not serving in the military. Obviously there are going to be times it is not fun. That it's going to be tough. But it's not like you can always go back and join the military and be around such a closely bonded, driven group of people like this later in life."

Did Ensign Squires give a second thought for volunteering into possible war in 2012? "No," he said, "because when I signed up, I knew what I was doing. I knew what I got myself into."

PREPARING TO BE THEIR BEST

There couldn't have been three more-prepared guys coming off a US college campus, outside of military academies. Squires, Hershaw, and Miller are products of one of the most physically and mentally demanding programs in American college sports.

The same month his three rowers became military officers, coach Michael Callahan led the Huskies to their first back-to-back national titles in more than seventy years. Callahan led UW to five IRA national championships in the first seven years he'd been Washington's head man. And he didn't get there by comforting his guys with blankets, cookies and warm milk when times got tough.

"The Marine Corps' ethos and that of UW are the same: No excuses," Miller said.

It wasn't uncommon at Conibear Shellhouse near dawn for some of UW's finest-conditioned athletes to throw up from utter exhaustion during morning workouts. Then drive on.

"Mike runs the program like a professional," added Miller.

"That's what I admire about the Marine Corps, too."

Sure enough, Washington's men's crew team won each of their five finals races at the IRAs that June, while setting course records, as clean a sweep from freshmen through varsity eight as the storied sport of crew had ever seen.

"When the call comes, you have to perform. That's true whether it's the IRAs or on a mission overseas," said Miller, who grew up in Woodbridge, Virginia, fifteen minutes from the Marine Corps Base Quantico. His mother worked as an administrator there, in-processing and out-processing Marines, and he had an uncle who served in Vietnam. "Washington rowing expects the best of the best. So do the Marines. They both expect you to be a man."

Callahan and Husky rowing helped Miller become that man. Crew turned Miller from a formerly self-described "hella skinny," six-foot-two, 150-pound freshman football player in high school into the supremely conditioned, Division-I athlete.

"It's the team concept," he said. "On multiple occasions when we were out there in the mornings doing PT (physical training), some guys really got after it, went to where they puked. Then they kept going. You knew where your limits were and could push past it. And you could get up the next day and do it again. That was what was expected in the crew program at Washington. And that's what is expected in the Marines."

As Squires put it, what he learned in Callahan's program is that "You can't stop. You can't give up. There are other guys counting on you to put out maximum effort. It's not worth it to give into the pain. The rewards far outweigh the cost of giving up."

These parallels in mental toughness and sense of duty between Husky crew and the military isn't exactly a coincidence. The ties between the two institutions run deep.

In 1923 Washington, led by coach and 1914-15 Husky rower Rusty Callow, surprised the favored US Naval Academy to win the Huskies' first IRA national title. Max Luft, Charles Dunn, Fred Spuhn, captain Sam Shaw, Pat Tidmarsh, Rowland France, Harry John Dutton, Dow Walling, and Don Grant were inducted into the Husky Hall of Fame in 1990.

Callow then coached the Navy rowing team from 1950

until his retirement in 1959. His Midshipmen, eight-man crew won gold at the 1952 Helsinki Olympics. Four years later Callow was inducted into the National Rowing Hall of Fame in Mystic, Connecticut.

Likewise, UW's coach Callahan grew up basically steeped in water and discipline because of his dad, a 1962 graduate of the Naval Academy at Annapolis, Maryland. "He was always on ships, at least most of the time. So I grew up near the water, for sure," the younger Callahan said. "When I was growing up, lots of my friends were in the Navy, and one of my best friends growing up, his dad was a commercial fisherman. So I was always scrubbing the bottoms of boats or rowing around."

Callahan became a champion rower at the world junior and Under 23 championships during the 1990s, then a member of the US Olympic rowing team as a spare in 2004.

Long ago he noticed the bent of a rower leans toward the military. That is, they share an edge. "Rowers inherently have a chip on their shoulder," Callahan said. "But I try not to foster that. That makes us different (as Huskies). I want them to be the best that they can be with what they can control. I want them to be something else."

TOUGHENING UP FOR THE REAL WORLD

That demand on being special is what drove Squires, Hershaw, and Miller to UW rowing, and then into the Navy and the Marines.

"When you row at the University of Washington, you are expected to produce your finest product at any given moment," Hershaw said. "We all had our best moments at the national championships. That was special.

"It's good to know you can push yourself past the standard of excellence, whether it's in rowing, the military, in training, as a student. It's too easy to give in and say, 'I can't.' To be able to push past that is special. Not a lot of people get to

> **"You knew where your limits were and could push past it. And you could get up the next day and do it again. That was what was expected in the crew program at Washington. And that's what is expected in the Marines."**
>
> C.J. MILLER

experience that. Now, in my daily life, I expect myself to be better than the average person. Not to brag, but just inside, with my character."

The Squires family furthers UW's link with the Navy through crew.

Rob Squires was a three-year letter winner in football and won four letters in crew at Episcopal High School in Jacksonville, Florida. His father, Steve Squires, is a former US Navy Captain and pilot, but Rob said his dad "was pretty much hands off as far as what I wanted to do."

Still, the former officer's son earned a full ROTC scholarship to Washington beginning in 2009, four years after Captain Squires resigned his commission from the Navy.

As for how the younger Squires got into rowing, that wasn't exactly scientific. He Googled "college rowing programs," then inquired to the first twenty schools that popped onto his computer screen. "Next thing I knew, I was at Washington," he said. "I wanted to be pushed among the best in the country...I knew I didn't want to work in any cubicle all day, every day. I wanted to see the world."

While Miller and Hershaw waited more than a year to begin their military careers because of the American troop pullouts in Iraq and Afghanistan, Miller went to coach crew at St. John College High School near his home in the Washington, D.C., area.

Hershaw sought internships back east, perhaps in national security. He earned his political science degree from the University of Washington with a focus on international security, and the strategic and intelligence aspects of the military and the government intrigued him. His father, Cam, was a Marine corporal before retiring from active duty. Three of four uncles were Marines. His mother is an elementary school teacher back home in Washougal, Washington, across the Columbia River from Oregon.

Hershaw, whose sister rowed at UW beginning in 2002,

UW men's eight leads Cornell (foreground) in the 2013 Windermere Cup. Note "Class of 1961" written on their handles to honor the group that donated the oars to UW crew.

took six-week-leadership cycles over each of the 2010 and '11 summers in a program for candidates to become an officer without being fully in the ROTC program. The Marines taught him land navigation and basic military courtesies and histories. Basically, Hershaw said, the course was designed to "stress you out" with sleep deprivation, menial tasks such as making and re-making a bed, plus more yelling than a crew coach alongside a training boat.

"It wasn't fun, but it wasn't too bad," he said. "I was used to waking up early, working out hard and then going to class. A lot of guys weren't. They would fall asleep in class, all worn out. I mean, honestly, after going through freshman year with [Huskies' crew freshman coach] Luke McGee, you are used to that stuff."

Miller, who earned his UW degree in physiology, remembered exactly where he was sitting in his class on September 11, 2001. He remembers watching television later with his sixth-grade classmates, as family friends working in the nearby Pentagon were hit by one of the jets terrorists hijacked and crashed that horrific morning.

"You can't have a national tragedy like that and not be affected in some way," he said. "As I got older, I knew I had to get out there and do something."

Miller graduated from UW wanting to either be an infantry Marine officer or serve in an amphibious assault unit after officer basic school in 2013. He chose the Marines over the Army, Navy, or Air Force, because he liked its macho missions and reputation. its "warrior culture."

Squires, who went aboard *USS Michael Murphy* in Maine weeks after that 2012 IRA national title, was thinking before he left UW about being in charge of a few dozen enlisted sailors, their pay, their welfare, their performance evaluations—their lives.

"Definitely I'm humbled and nervous. And I'm excited, as well," he said just before he left his elite, driven, supremely tough team at UW for another. "It's not something that everyone does. I realize that. To be defending our country, it's really humbling." ∎

Photo: Scott Eklund/Red Box Pictures

A Regatta So Loud You Can Feel It

2013 poster

S EAMUS LABRUM surprised his parents in 2009. The teenager decided to break free from his native East Coast to be a coxswain for the University of Washington's national powerhouse rowing program.

When Labrum made his decision, his coach at Holy Spirit High School in Cape May, New Jersey, took a poster off his office wall and gave it to the newest Washington Husky. That poster commemorated the Windermere Cup.

"My high school coach had coached at Penn, and he had the poster from when he was there," Labrum said. "That's when I learned it's a pretty big deal here. It's special, the Windermere Cup."

Before packing up his high-school coach's Cup poster and enrolling at Washington, the then high-school-senior coxswain barked at the United States' national four in the grand final of the 2011 World Rowing Under 23 Championships in Amsterdam. A year later he coxed the US men's four to a silver medal at the 2012 World Rowing Under 23 Championships in Lithuania.

The 2013 Windermere Cup race was Labrum's fourth and final Windermere Cup. In 2013 he also won gold for UW at the Head of the Charles Regatta in Boston, and then beat the host graduate students of Cambridge on the famed "Boat Race" course along the Thames in London.

Yet, to him, nothing compares to the Windermere Cup. It's, well...poster-worthy.

Said Labrum from the Windermere Dining Room of UW's Conibear Shellhouse three days before the twenty-seventh Cup, "I've also been to Henley to race, but as a competitor, there is nothing like the Windermere Cup."

It's the lay of the land that makes the Montlake Cut—and

In 2013 the Huskies celebrate winning the Windermere Cup with the winner's flag and a row back to the shell house.

thus the Windermere Cup—so unique. And so loud.

ROWING TO THE ROAR OF THE CROWD

The banks on either side of the Cut form a narrow channel in which no more than four boats can race through safely at one time. That proximity from shore puts fans far closer to the rowers—within a couple dozen yards—than most rowing venues that feature open water and require binoculars for adequate viewing of a race.

Viewing the Windermere Cup through binoculars inside the Cut would afford the viewer a close-up of the rowers' pores.

It is, in effect, stadium crew racing.

"Nothing comes as close to racing inside a stadium," Labrum said. "All the boats, all the people lining the Cut, screaming and cheering. They drown me out. It's exhilarating."

Michael Callahan knows the energy of the Windermere Cup. He's lived it.

Callahan is a former conference- and world-champion rower for UW. Then he became the coach of UW's men's crew program and led it to unprecedented heights. "When you are warming up behind all the yachts, you can feel it," Callahan said.

"Then when you come around the yachts to line up and look down the Cut, a tingle goes down your spine."

Callahan led Washington's men's crew to become the first team to win five consecutive Intercollegiate Rowing Association (IRA) men's varsity eight national titles. They had also won twelve of the last fourteen Windermere Cups entering the thirtieth regatta in 2016.

Labrum's job as coxswain was to make the stroke calls through that energy inside the Montlake Cut and keep his eight rowers in perfect harmony for under six minutes across all 2,000 meters of the course.

That's relatively easy during practices; UW trains at dawn in front of a few geese and maybe a shoreline jogger or biker. It's an entirely different challenge for a coxswain to make his calls over tens of thousands of screaming spectators, their blaring yacht horns, and the Husky Band rockin' from the finish line. Those sounds echo off the banks of the Montlake Cut on race days.

ABOVE: Husky cheerleaders rally the crowds from ship to shore to support their rowing teams.

Photos, top left & right: Scott Eklund/Red Box Pictures; Photo left: Red Box Pictures

ABOVE:
Seamus Labrum and his teammates accept the winners' Cup and wear their first-place medals after the 2013 Windermere Cup.

LEFT:
Yachts pass through the Montlake Cut for the boat parade following the Windermere Cup races.

"It's just insanely loud," said Todd Kennett, coach for Cornell's men's team, who also raced for the Big Red.

Kennett said the Montlake Cut crowd might as well be a Seattle Seahawks NFL crowd.

"We couldn't hear the coxswain, so someone had to knock on the side of the boat to make a call." He and his Cornell crewmates came in second to Washington for the 1991 Windermere Cup.

"As awesome as many events go, this may be one of the premier ones," Kennett said. "Just the way it's set up, the course, the fans, and how fair it is for everyone to race, it's definitely an event like no other. It's unreal."

With all those cheers for the Huskies, it was no wonder UW's varsity eight men were 21-3 in Windermere Cup final races from 1991 through 2015.

"It's pure adrenaline for the guys, with all that noise in the Cut. You can definitely feel it," said Labrum, who coxed the men's "A" boat that won the varsity four in the 2012 Windermere Cup. "If I don't call a split, the power in the boat still goes up."

Rather than throw up his arms and enjoy the ride, Labrum and his fellow coxswains have technology on their side.

"Now we've got the speaker system," Labrum said with a wry smile. "I can turn it up to eleven so they can hear me."

HOSTING AN ALL-AMERICAN REGATTA

The 2013 Regatta was only the tenth time over twenty-seven Windermere Cups in which UW men's and women's teams faced the same opponents: Cornell and Dartmouth. In addition, those schools brought their junior-varsity eight teams, adding depth that year.

Ernst, Callahan, and Windermere had wanted to bring top Ivy League crews to the Cup for years. Because Cornell's and Dartmouth's own annual rivalry event had been scheduled for late in the 2013 rowing season, toward June, UW invited them both to Seattle and had them race each other as well as the Huskies.

That's why 2013 was the only year in the Cup's history to not have an international entry. (The 2014 and '15 Cups welcomed the veteran, Olympic-quality national teams of Great Britain and New Zealand, respectively.)

Ryan Ganong, Dartmouth's senior captain in 2013, was as pumped as he was honored—and awed—to be rowing in his first Windermere Cup.

"We see Washington every year at the IRAs in New Jersey, and we are really blown away by their rowing," Ganong said. "We aspire to be like them. It's a huge privilege to be racing out there [in Seattle]."

> " It's just insanely loud…
> We couldn't hear the coxswain, so
> someone has to knock on the side of
> the boat to make a call. "
>
> TODD KENNETT

ADDING MORE TO THE RACES THAN ROWING

If you've never been to a Windermere Cup and you are anywhere near Seattle on the first Saturday in May, you owe it to yourself to grab a spot along the Montlake Cut. And not just for the final races. There is far more to each Cup.

Before Labrum and his Huskies got their chance to race in the 2013 Cup, over 800 athletes—from kids to masters visiting from British Columbia to California—raced in this annual, mega-regatta.

The first race signal went off at 9:55 a.m. for the men's eight boats, which featured fifty-plus-year-olds. Participating teams included those from legendary Puget Sound boat designer Pocock Racing, from Sammamish and Vashon Island, Washington, and Willamette, Oregon.

The University of British Columbia entered a boat for the women's college open eight race at 10:31, as did the University of Portland. The University of Victoria in B.C. was in the women's freshman eight race at 11 a.m., while Lake Oswego, Oregon, was in the Referee Cup, the boys' high school eight, at 10:52.

When Labrum commanded the number-one-ranked UW men's varsity eight boat to stare down Dartmouth, Cornell, and the tens of thousands of fans that lined the 2,000-meter course in 2013, the weather was an idyllic 70 degrees Fahrenheit and sunny, with little wind.

The Windermere Cup

Members of the Husky Marching Band add their horns to the cacophony of noise during the races.

is a rockin' event when it's raining, blowing, and 50 degrees. One can imagine the rager on the Cut when it's warm and sunny.

"And all for the right price," Ernst said.

The Windermere Cup is one of the largest free public events in the Northwest. Windermere Real Estate spends hundreds of thousands of dollars per year putting on the event, while the Seattle Yacht Club pays for the log boom where swarms of boaters tie up to watch the Cup races and the boat parade, which follows the race. The yacht club also pays the resulting overtime costs for Seattle Police Depart-

Boats of all sizes swarm toward Lake Washington in the Opening Day parade once the Windermere Cup races are complete.

ment officers to patrol and secure the event, and for the Seattle Fire Department to inspect event sites.

But for you and me, it's all free.

"The most important thing is that it's part of the fabric of the community," said UW's Ernst. "Seattle is an outdoor-sports community. It's still a work-hard community. The people identify with rowing in our part of the country in a different way than football or basketball, but they see rowing as one of the parts of our culture. And the Windermere Cup is a hallmark for that sport." ■

Per tradition, when a boat wins the race, the crew tosses their coxswain into the water to celebrate. Here the British men's crew performs the coxswain toss after winning the 2014 Windermere Cup.

Photo: Windermere Real Estate Services Company

CHAPTER TWELVE

How UW's Huskies Impressed the Brits

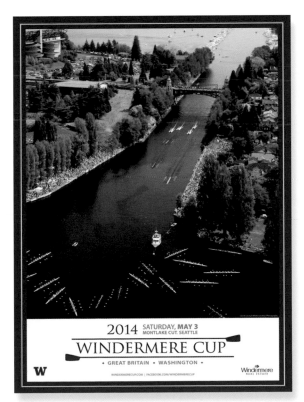

2014 poster

O**N THE** warmest May 1 in Seattle's history, a most impressive lineup of students and athletes gathered at the annual athletes' dinner for the twenty-eighth Windermere Cup.

The rowers, representing Washington's and Great Britain's champion men's and women's national teams, were majoring or had degrees in physics, astronomy, mathematics, speech and language sciences, and environmental sciences. Some had already graduated from Oxford and Cambridge. Two from the British women's eight were finishing their PhDs.

Nathaniel Reilly O'Donnell was a twenty-six-year-old with a law degree from University College London.

He'd been rowing since he was twelve and was a world junior champion in a four-man boat in 2006. He'd been an alternate on Great Britain's team that led all of the 2012 London Games by winning nine medals.

O'Donnell rowed again in the twenty-eighth Windermere Cup on May 3, 2014, and at that June's European championships and August's World Rowing Championships with not one or two, but four herniated disks in his back and neck.

"Is there any reason to not be proud of these athletes?" Bob Ernst asked at that Cup's athletes' dinner at the school's Conibear Shellhouse, after temperatures soared to 85 degrees and made an already cordial week even warmer.

Ernst had just passed a microphone around the crew house's dining room, allowing each of the rowers on the four teams that raced through the Montlake Cut for that Windermere Cup to introduce themselves and tell of their interests.

There was even a man knighted by British royalty present for this particular Cup athletes' dinner, which included a keynote speech by Judy Rantz Willman, the daughter of

Joe Rantz, who rowed on the Huskies eight—the "boys in the boat" that stunned the world by winning gold at the 1936 Berlin Olympics in front of Adolph Hitler.

"Little did I know when I was given *The Boys in the Boat* to read last year—I thought, 'Oh, no, not another rowing book'—that I would be so inspired by the history of this place," said Sir David Tanner, the performance director for British Rowing who led Great Britain's delegation to Seattle for that year's Cup.

Willman was a neighbor in the Seattle suburb of Redmond, Washington, to Daniel James Brown, the author of the popular *The Boys in the Boat* about the 1936 Huskies' rowing team. Willman told Brown her father's story, and that of the kids from the Depression winning gold as college students, and Brown turned it into a book for which a movie was being planned.

After Willman described the rowers in *The Boys in the Boat*, she told that year's Huskies and British team members that, in a sport where work ethic and harmony are paramount, "You are all made of the same stuff. You become a better person because you are always improving what you are. These life lessons are a part of you, just as [they were] for the 'boys in the boat' in 1936."

UNDERESTIMATING THE COMPETITION

The British were going to bring younger, more-novice national crews to the twenty-eighth Windermere Cup.

Then the Brits remembered the Huskies. They remembered what their UW hosts did to them in July 2013 at their famed Royal

> **"Little did I know when I was given *The Boys in the Boat* to read last year—I thought, 'Oh, no, not another rowing book'—that I would be so inspired by the history of this place."**
>
> SIR DAVID TANNER

For each year's Windermere Cup, ribbons are printed with all competing crews' names and tied to glass medals awarded for first, second, and third place.

Henley Regatta on the River Thames outside London.

The British men—the winningest program at the previous Olympics, a systematic machine UW director of rowing and Olympic-winning coach Bob Ernst calls the world's finest rowing system—remembered Washington's varsity eight.

Those Huskies were the only collegians in the Grand Challenge Cup final regatta of national teams to equal Germany's previous record time in the Royal Henley. The veteran British had to set a new course record in the summer, of 2014 at Henley to beat the Huskies. That was the Huskies' first defeat since 2010. The loss came a month after UW won its third consecutive US national championship, its fourth in five years.

The Huskies left behind at Henley an enhanced reputation as one of the finest university programs not only in America, but in the world.

Plus, the British arrived in Seattle knowing the Windermere Cup's internationally renowned, one-of-a-kind setting, the sport's closest thing to rowing inside a football stadium. Tens of thousands of Northwest natives roaring on the close-set banks of the Montlake Cut—it's a raucous scene that would likely overwhelm newbie rowers. Even the vets admitted they hadn't seen anything like what awaited them in that Windermere Cup.

"We initially thought about a bit more of a development crew," said Rob Dauncey, the coach of Team Great Britain's men's eight. "But then when we thought and remembered about the tough racing Washington gave us at Henley (in 2014) where, in the Grand Challenge eight and the

Members of champion crews receive windbreakers commemorating the year the won the Windermere Cup.

Ladies Plate eight, we just managed to get past Washington. We thought maybe we ought to stiffen up our crew and, you know, give it a bit more power." The coach added with only a trace of a grin, "Obviously, as a national team, we sort of expect to win."

Britain had sent its national women's team to two previous Windermere Cups: in 1998, when it won, and in 2002, when it finished behind UW and Stanford. The 2014 event was the first time the British men's and women's teams competed at the same Windermere Cup.

Dauncey brought to Seattle an eight-man crew, which included six members of the Great Britain team that won in the 2013 World Rowing Championships.

Dauncey's crew was led by twenty-seven-year-old Daniel Ritchie, who won a gold medal at the 2013 World Rowing Championships.

This, as Ernst likes to say, was the real deal.

"This is the best competition we've had for a Windermere Cup since the very first one with the Soviets in 1987," Ernst said of the British before the 2014 race. "It is absolutely the best rowing program in the world."

By now, world champions wouldn't dare bring anything but their best to compete in the Windermere Cup.

"We've brought the best," Huskies' men's coach Michael Callahan said that year of the challenge facing his young team. At that point, UW's program had won five of the previous eight IRA national championships and in 2013 had

Representatives of Windermere Real Estate get the honor of bestowing the Cup on the 2014 men's eight champions, Great Britain.

swept all five grand finals—from freshman through JV and varsity—at them. The "best." The word befits this remarkable event. And its venue.

GETTING THE ROYAL TREATMENT

For the 2014 Cup, local volunteers escorted the British on a short shopping trip to Seattle's Northgate Mall. The University Book Store is also an annual favorite for visiting crews who like to stock up on Huskies' gear to take home. Great Britain's teams also enjoyed what their coaches called tremendous steaks at Daniel's Broiler on South Lake Union.

After Wednesday's training, they went on the "Crews' Cruise" sponsored by the Seattle Yacht Club, which took the visitors on private boats across Lake Washington, past the 520 bridge and, of course, close to Microsoft co-founder Bill Gates' lakeside estate. "Everyone wants to see Bill Gates'

house," said host Michele Shaw of the SYC.

That Thursday night the Huskies and British teams were back inside Conibear Shellhouse for the customary Windermere Cup athletes' dinner. They ate under the Husky Clipper, that "boys in the boat" shell from the 1936 Olympics.

Friday included more training and some free time. Friday is the night some veteran rowers have used to indulge in as much Seattle as they can get. Namely, the Australians. The 1996 Olympic champions partied their way through the week, only to get beaten by the Huskies in what remains the Windermere Cup's greatest upset.

But the British were under a strict training regimen, limiting their opportunity for too many shenanigans. Asked playfully if he might let his guys loose on Seattle for some fun that week, Britain's coach Dauncey allowed that "perhaps" there could be time for that. On Saturday night, after

UW's women perform their own coxswain toss despite coming in second to the Huskies.

the racing.

Windermere's OB Jacobi, standing next to Dauncey, showed he was a good Husky, one keenly interested in his home team continuing its domination. They'd won seven consecutive Windermere Cup championships, including eleven of the previous twelve. "If they want to go out Friday night," a smiling Jacobi told Dauncey, "we can certainly make that happen."

After years of winning the Windermere Cup by ten seconds or more, that 2014 Huskies' men's crew, a team ranked number one in US college rowing, lost to Great Britain's veteran—and apparently rested—eight-man crew by two seconds, or about six seats.

But UW's sixth-ranked women's eight beat the British women by more than four seconds, garnering a Windermere Cup split. ■

Community Support Gives the Cup Local Flavor

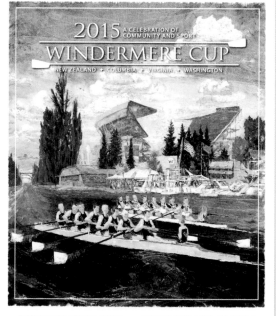

2015 poster

BOB ERNST believes the Windermere Cup succeeds because of how the regatta relates to the fabric of the Pacific Northwest's culture.

Specifically, the region's civic-mindedness.

Despite the international prestige the Windermere Cup has earned by hosting the world's best crews for thirty years (and counting), the Cup has retained its grassroots Seattle feel. That's because Windermere Real Estate is a Seattle-born and -centered company and so many Northwest home-buyers have used its services.

The world's best rowers come to the University of Washington and the Montlake Cut to compete the first Saturday in May for an event that remains a relatively community-based, locally funded effort. Almost every aspect of the Windermere Cup is essentially a cooperative enterprise.

It starts with Windermere Real Estate.

Windermere grew from only eight agents in 1972 to more than 7,000 agents by 2016, and a network of 300 franchised offices throughout the West Coast and including Mexico, making it the largest regional real estate company in the Western US.

Each of its offices contributes money to put on the annual Windermere Cup. In the early days of the first Cups, some owners from smaller offices outside Puget Sound didn't want to contribute to an event in Seattle, which has become increasingly expensive as the number of media outlets and competing sports options has exploded since the 1980s. But as the event grew in status and renown far beyond the city to across the nation and the world, franchisees generally embraced their role in making the Windermere Cup a success.

"It took time," Windermere founder John Jacobi said. "We brought in all of our owners (back in the late 1980s) and

Photo: Scott Eklund/Red Box Pictures

An official waves his flag to signal the start of the 2015 Windermere Cup race.

told them this is what we are going to do."

Collecting money from franchisees got easier as franchise owners saw how it benefited the entire region and, thus, their own reputations up and down the West Coast. The regatta attracts crews of various ages, from teenagers to seniors, who compete in races that start hours before the Windermere Cup men's and women's finals. Many of these rowers were, are, or may become Windermere customers.

"I think it's another part of our branding," said OB Jacobi, John Jacobi's son and the eventual Windermere president. "Can't do the Windermere Cup any better than we've done it for the last twenty years. The first three years were a little iffy, but now we've got all our ducks in a row."

Windermere pays for the international flights, meals, and hotels for team parties of about twenty-five each year. Teams used to stay in UW's dorms, but the massive housing shortage on campus pushed the visiting rowers off campus, usually to the Silver Cloud Inn north of UW. The company also pays for the week of team events, boat tours, dinners, even a grade-school rowing clinic held at Conibear Shellhouse in conjunction with the Cup. Windermere can even offer participating crews gifts, the same way NCAA rules allow college football teams to receive gifts from bowl games played postseason.

"They are sponsored, just like any other team," Ernst said of the visiting rowers.

Windermere estimates another $150,000-200,000 worth of employee time is spent annually to put on the Cup. No revenue is collected, nor financial profit gained, from the event. Occasionally Windermere recruits sponsors from outside the company to support features that enhance the regatta, such as a Jumbotron video scoreboard that Windermere had installed along the Montlake Cut for several years' races to relay action occurring down the course.

How much does Windermere spend each year on the Cup for a sport that isn't football or basketball or exactly mainstream anywhere else but perhaps in Seattle, Boston, and

> ❝ **There are twelve-, fifteen-year-old kids who probably wouldn't have started rowing at all had they not seen the Windermere Cup.** ❞
>
> JOHN W. JACOBI

England?

"Hundreds of thousands of dollars each year," said both Jacobi and his sister Jill Jacobi Wood, Windermere co-president. Why? "It feels really good," Jill Jacobi Wood said.

As Ernst likes to say, the Windermere Cup is "the greatest free event around."

BRINGING THE BOOM

The delivering and installing of the log booms that form the start of the 2,000-meter course in Union Bay is a community effort.

The Seattle Yacht Club pays for the log boom on Lake Washington, and not just its installation. Those logs come from Shelton, Washington, above Olympia on the southern end of the Olympic Peninsula. Leaving before dawn, a tugboat and its operator spend all day navigating their barge of logs northward, from the bottom of Puget Sound to Seattle. Once the barge reaches Union Bay, cranes from Mason Construction of Seattle install the logs along both sides of the race course near the starting line.

The log boom is set in place by Thursday night, so by Friday morning boaters angle for their preferred mooring along the boom. Friday is a notorious "hooky day" from work for many Northwest boat owners, because space on the boom is first-come, first-served. That's how swarms of boats and yachts tie up for "course-side" viewing of each Windermere Cup race and the boat parade that follows.

The boat parade reverses the rowing course, starting west of the Montlake Cut and finishing beyond the log boom, so these boaters become the unofficial judges for the decorated yachts in the parade.

After the cost of the log boom skyrocketed, UW asked for a modest donation from the boat owners to offset the increased costs. UW suggested a donation of ten dollars per foot of beam width, which includes any dinghy that must be tied to the craft's bow.

The SYC agreed to pay for the overtime accrued by the Seattle Police Department officers, who patrol and secure each Windermere Cup Regatta, and for the Seattle Fire Department officials to inspect sites.

The Windermere Cup is not a college football bowl game or basketball tournament. The Cup is not in the megabucks world of nationally televised college sports and the inherent moneymaking and pseudo-professionalism of that world.

Rowers don't compete to make millions in a pro league. They compete for the love of, and dedication to, their sport.

"Some of us were rowers, but most of us weren't. We appreciate the sport for what it is," Jacobi said. "This is...'pure' isn't the right word...It's not like Bob Ernst is making three

million a year."

Ernst, the former University of Washington director of rowing, got a huge laugh from that. "I'm waiting for it," he said, while sitting next to Jacobi in 2014. "John, I can have you help me."

The sense of community and cooperation that make the Windermere Cup unique didn't start off that way.

Content with how the Opening Day boat parade existed for years, SYC members took a while to accept the event's expansion by folks who were, to them, outsiders.

"It used to be the Opening Day boat parade, and eventu-

COMMUNITY

The Kids of Windermere Cup

A few days before each Windermere Cup Regatta, Windermere Real Estate invites kids to spend a day with rowers from the University of Washington and visiting crew teams as part of its annual community outreach event, Windermere Cup KidsCrew.

In 2015, fifth-graders from Seattle's Martin Luther King Elementary, got to spend the day with New Zealand World Champion and UW National Champion rowing teams. The children were taken on a short tour, starting with a visit to the Alaska Airlines Arena to see the Husky Hall of Fame.

"I don't think we've ever heard 'This is so cool!' so many times as we did at that moment," said Shelley Rossi, Vice President of Communications for Windermere Real Estate. "The real fun began when we let them all loose inside the UW football stadium."

The kids got to race each other on rowing machines, and even climbed into a shell on the water. The athletes talked about stretching and exercising issues, and fielded questions

about nutrition from their eager audience. Each child was also fed lunch and given a Windermere Cup poster for rowers to sign as a memento of their special day.

As Rossi explains, "The significance of an experience like this might be lost on some of us, but for these kids it can be life changing.

A day like this allows their dreams to grow, dreams they can one day achieve. Whether it's rowing at UW, becoming a doctor, or just attending college, days like this remind these kids that it's all possible." ■

ally they got rowing races roped into it, and now that has morphed into the Windermere Cup," Jacobi said, explaining the coordination of efforts for the first Windermere Cups. "It took a while, but now it's perfect, and they know we aren't going do anything crazy. They accept the Windermere Cup for what it is. And what it is, is bringing the best rowing teams in the world here to compete."

INFLUENCING GENERATION UPON GENERATION

Generations of children in Seattle have grown up sitting on the banks of the Cut to watch the Windermere Cup as fans, or while working with their real-estate parents to support

Boats arrive from many countries to enjoy the spectacle of the Windermere Cup while docked along log booms paid for by the Seattle Yacht Club.

Photos: Windermere Real Estate Services Company

the event, or even as competitors in the Cups themselves.

"There are twelve- to fifteen-year-old kids who probably wouldn't have started rowing at all had they not seen the Windermere Cup," Jacobi said. "There are a number of strong junior rowing programs in the area, [like] Pocock. A lot of Windermere kids are in those."

Jacobi himself never rowed competitively, but two of John Jacobi's granddaughters earned a collegiate crew scholarship.

Each year, hundreds of athlete rowers—from kids to juniors to masters—race in the regatta. They come from Bellingham, Portland, Olympia, British Columbia, and beyond. One Windermere Cup included Hawaiian outrigger canoes. That has added to the Pacific Northwest's rich rowing

Rowers sign Windermere Cup posters for the elementary students who came for KidsCrew, an annual community-outreach event sponsored by Windermere Real Estate.

heritage, which dates back long before George Pocock began building boats in Seattle in 1911.

Windermere's partner in putting on the regatta, the SYC, has ties with Seattle's boating community leading back to the nineteenth century. The SYC originated in 1892, making it one of the nation's longer-running yacht clubs. Through its partnership with the Pacific Northwest boating community, and later the Windermere Cup, SYC is one of the nation's more community-active yacht clubs.

SYC's predecessor, the Elliott Bay Yacht Club, hosted a regatta of boats on Independence Days as early as 1895. In 1909, when Seattle hosted the Alaska-Yukon Exposition on what was to become the UW campus, the SYC was the official host for visiting boaters. SYC's commodore and members conducted a public "Potlatch Parade" at SYC's clubhouse, then in West Seattle.

By 1913, Seattle was hosting an Opening Day Regatta and boat parade in Elliott Bay off the downtown waterfront. In 1920, after SYC relocated its facilities from West Seattle to Portage Bay, south of the UW campus, the route for the Opening Day Parade and Regatta was moved to the Montlake Cut.

"Opening Day (is) Seattle's annual opportunity to renew its connection to the water and for friends and family to experience world-class festivities under gorgeous, open skies," Seattle mayor Ed Murray wrote in a 2014 welcome letter that kicked off the twenty-eighth annual Windermere Cup.

"Whether you're on the water celebrating from the log boom or relaxing on shore, please enjoy the pride and sense of community that sets Opening Day and our spectacular city apart."

So does this: Seattle's Opening Day boating festivities have survived both World Wars. By 2015 they'd run for ninety-five uninterrupted years.

In 1959, SYC named "Hell's a Poppin'" as the logo for the boat parade, beginning the annual tradition of SYC assigning a theme to Opening Day. Each year the boat parade begins promptly at noon with the blast of a cannon and the raising of Montlake's drawbridge, sending hundreds of fans, who watched the races from above, scurrying off the bridge.

SYC puts on a drama production the Wednesday before each Windermere Cup, and on Thursday evening it hosts a happy hour "rope-yarn," an annual celebration at its

A formidable team (from left to right): Michael Callahan, Jill Jacobi Wood, Bob Ernst, Seattle Yacht Club officer Sally Cole, OB Jacobi, Seattle Yacht Club officers Tom Wingard and Ted Shultz, and Geoff Wood.

headquarters located on the southeast edge of Portage Bay. Fridays before the Cup the local antique- and classic-boat society sponsors tours of the log boom at the end of the Cut, and then there are dinners and dancing at various SYC venues.

"Although we call it 'Opening Day,'" said one-time SYC Admiral Michael Carrosino, "it really is a week-long event and civic celebration of our boating heritage, with many fun-filled activities."

In the 2010s, Windermere and UW even started hosting a media race along the 2,000-meter course through Montlake Cut. Matt Lacey, executive director of the Pocock Rowing Center on Portage Bay in Seattle, a few long strokes from the west end of the Montlake Cut, presented the crystal trophy to Seattle's KOMO television for winning the 2014 Windermere Cup media race.

Photo: Windermere Real Estate Services Company

"The Windermere Cup and opening of the boating season is fantastic," Lacey said. "It's like Christmas in Seattle for rowing."

CONTINUING THE COMMUNITY LEGACY

After decades of providing a civic boat parade only for Seattle, the SYC and Windermere Real Estate have blended together a world-class rowing regatta and a grand boating day unlike any other.

"We have a perfect relationship with the Seattle Yacht Club," Jacobi said. "They don't want [the Cup] to be a commercial enterprise. They feel really strongly about that. And that's good, because all three of us are comfortable about that."

The Huskies certainly are.

"The most important thing is [the Cup's] part of the fabric of the community," UW's Ernst said.

At the athletes' dinner on the eve of the 2015 Windermere Cup, the same year that welcomed New Zealand's national team, Columbia University, and the University of Virginia,

Jacobi's children donated a shell to Washington's crew program. The boat was named the *John W. Jacobi*, in honor of the company patriarch's retirement from Windermere Real Estate, and was christened on the docks of UW's Conibear Shellhouse while all those Kiwis and Ivy League students watched from the patios overhead.

The *John W. Jacobi* has since been used by visiting international men's crews for the final race of each year's Cup.

"We hope that people identify our company with, in this particular case, what a great sport rowing is," John Jacobi said.

"It's world class. It has world status," Ernst said. "And it fits within the fabric of our community. And I think, like John says, it's part of the branding of the company, and the company is the community. That's why everybody buys in. That's why the yacht club buys in. Because all of us, we are performing for the community. That's my sense of what it is."

"Plus," Jacobi added, "it's a lot of fun. It's really a blast." ∎

Building on Tradition

Founded in 1892, Seattle Yacht Club is one of our country's most active and long-established yacht clubs. Since the 1920 move to Portage Bay, the Seattle Yacht Club Opening Day event has been celebrated yearly—ninety-five years as of 2015.

Seattle Yacht Club Opening Day Committee has sixty-plus sub-committees working in tandem from October to the day of the event on the first Saturday in May. This constitutes hundreds of volunteers freely giving their time to this very successful event.

The Montlake Cut had always been a favorite rowing venue, and from the day it opened, Husky crews had practiced and competed there. In 1976 log booms were used on both sides of the course extending nearly to Webster Point, allowing flat water for the Olympic-standard 2,000-meter rowing course. And so was born another tradition: boats started tying up to these log booms on Friday to secure their prime parade and race viewing on Saturday.

In 1971 the SYC committee, then headed by former UW Athletic Director Ray Eckman, invited Huskies crew coach Dick Erickson to stage a rowing race to precede the big parade on Opening Day. Many SYC members have rowed and/or coached, so have a close association with crew.

Years later, SYC member John Jacobi teamed up with coaches Erickson and Ernst to create a new challenge. Thus began the Windermere Cup. Each year the most prominent crews, international, national, and local crews compete in what is described as the premier rowing venue in the world. ∎

UW's Stewards
of the Windermere Cup

2007 poster

BOB ERNST isn't all about crew. At Washington and around the Windermere Cup, it only seems like he is.

He arrived at Washington when Gerald Ford was president and the Windermere Cup was thirteen years from even starting. At that time, the Opening Day of Seattle's boating season had a boat parade, and the Huskies added to the regatta by staging a relatively non-descript race against a local opponent. That was in 1974.

Before he got to UW, Ernst was a center on Orange Coast College's national junior-college championship football team in 1963. He played that title game at the Rose Bowl, about an hour north of where he grew up in Costa Mesa, California. He also swam and competed in water polo while at Orange Coast for two years, then transferred to nearby UC Irvine. He continued swimming and water polo at Irvine,

plus he joined the Anteaters' fledgling rowing program in 1966 and '67.

In 1974 Ernst was twenty-seven and coaching his alma mater's crew. Huskies' iconic rowing coach Dick Erickson was impressed with how Ernst's Anteaters almost upset Washington that spring—so impressed that he offered Ernst a job as coach of the UW's freshmen men's team that fall.

Ernst accepted.

Bob Ernst first reached the elite level of international women's rowing in 1976 when, while still Erickson's assistant with the UW men's crew, he coached the United States' women's doubles scull at the Montreal Olympics.

By 1980 he succeeded John Lind as the coach of Washington's women's team. That had started in 1969 as a club sport, in 1975 became an intercollegiate varsity sport, and in 1977 was allowed into the previously all-male Varsity Boat Club

Former UW rowing coach Bob Ernst giving the press an interview on the docks of Conibear Shellhouse.

for the first time. How good and how immediately was Ernst a leader?

His first season in charge of the women's program in 1981, the Huskies' varsity and junior-varsity crews won national championships. They did that for the five consecutive years thereafter, too.

He also remained the US women's Olympic crew coach for the 1980 Moscow Games (which the Americans eventually boycotted), the 1984 Los Angeles Games (where Ernst won gold again), and for the 1988 Seoul Olympics.

In 1987 Ernst's women's teams at Washington won the varsity eight, junior-varsity eight, and varsity four national titles. So when Erickson decided to retire in 1987 after twenty years leading the UW men's program, Ernst was his obvious choice to replace him.

"It took me ten years to win a national championship when I took over the guys' team in 1987," Ernst said in his office at Conibear Shellhouse one spring afternoon before yet another rowing practice. "Let's just say both programs needed to be overhauled at the time," he added, referring to the UW men back in '87 and the women's team when he took it over again in 2007.

In 2007, after two more national championships with the guys, Ernst put himself in charge of the women's program again. That same year, as the university's director of rowing, he made former Husky rower and international champion Michael Callahan the men's head coach.

BRINGING UP A FORMER OLYMPIC HUSKY

Callahan rowed for Ernst at Washington from 1992-96. He won gold medals at the world junior and Nations Cup (now referred to as the Under-23 championship) that decade. Callahan then made the 2004 US Olympic team as a spare.

He was thirty-two when Ernst named him the head coach of the Huskies' men's program in 2007. That program first started 106 years earlier, in the spring of 1901, with the UW's first Class Day races between freshmen, sophomore, junior, and senior crews just off the shores of campus.

It's fitting that Callahan is comfortable with both a fast training pace and maintaining UW's rowing legacy through

A hangar built in 1918 for the Aviation Training Corps, but never used, was handed over to UW after WWI and used as a shell house for rowing crews.

the Windermere Cup and beyond. This former Navy brat knows a fast pace. Before he got to Washington, he was at *Bloomberg News*. Next he held a temporary job at Goldman Sachs. He was on the US Olympic rowing team. He then made a cross-country move for a coaching internship at his alma mater, UW.

In summers he competed against Harvard, California, Wisconsin, and other national powers in recruiting the world's top teenage rowers; UW's 2014 men's roster included natives of England, Italy, Slovenia, Australia, Canada, Croatia, Germany, New Zealand, and even Phoenix.

"Rowing is a very European-centric sport. Plus, there is Australia, New Zealand, and other spots. So you see the youngest, best people in the world. And we've attracted some to the University of Washington," Callahan said.

Callahan spent much of the 2011 summer in Europe, first to coach the United States coxed four at the World Rowing Under 23 Championships in Amsterdam, and then to scout the World Rowing Junior Championships in Eton Dorney, Great Britain.

"I really enjoy the fact that, at the University of Washington, we can go get the best rower in his age [group] in the world. We are that attractive to him. It's interesting. They

> **"Competition is the best form of development. Our guys are ready to compete during and after going through this program. We teach comparison."**
>
> MICHAEL CALLAHAN

are attracted not only by the rowing, but the school, too. They say, 'I really like your computer engineering program. I really like your mathematics program.'"

That 2011 autumn, Callahan also found time to marry former Yale rower Joanna Hess, daughter of two-time Husky crew captain Mike Hess.

Some of the Huskies' rivals hold UW's foreign influx against the Dawgs, as if it is a liability.

Callahan sees the opposite. His goal in recruiting is simple: "Find a person who fits the mentality of how we do things."

And how they do things is unlike almost anywhere else.

DISCOVERING HIDDEN GEMS

"You know, the biggest challenge is always redeveloping the culture," Ernst explained. "Sometimes you can be a good athlete, but you have to have a significant number of them to where people train to win rather than just train to race. It's different. Changing the culture has been the biggest challenge. And finally—fortunately—we are getting enough really good athletes to have this change."

So where does he get these really good athletes?

Ernst has a secret to turning programs from in need of a boost into elite programs: basketball, volleyball, and swimming meets. Each year Ernst attends the Washington state high school championships in each of those sports. He's invited by coaches across the state who have driven, athletically gifted players who may not be getting a major college scholarship in their first sport.

Men such as Matt Zapell. Ernst found UW's six-foot-five senior for the 2011 season when Zapell was a two-time league champion in basketball and third-place finisher in Washington state hoops at Vashon Island High School.

Ernst loves those hidden gems. That's a reason he returned to leading Washington's women's program. By 2012, exactly 25 percent of his varsity-eight powerhouse women's team, ranked second in the NCAA, were walk-ons. He had an all-state volleyball player who also started in basketball, and he coached a top track runner who also played basketball. Each earned a scholarship as well as a place on the top boat at UW.

"And then the other six rowers are world-class rowers," Ernst said of that year's Huskies varsity eight. "To have 25 percent of your lineup as walk-ons—that doesn't happen in any other sport."

Ernst explained that one of the reasons he wanted to coach the women's team again after coaching the UW men for twenty years was because of these facts: In 2012, there were roughly eighty-five women's intercollegiate Division-I rowing teams and there were about twenty scholarships available for women in the sport at each of those schools.

"That's 1,700 full-ride scholarships every year," Ernst said. "I'm here to tell you that there aren't 1,700 blue-chip recruits every year, and so it is an extremely interesting puzzle to solve. I'm a solver. I'm a builder," Ernst said, smiling. "I love that."

On any dark winter day, walk through Conibear's ground floor, just off the boat garage, or inside the football weight room in Graves

UW rowing coach Michael Callahan carries on the winning tradition for Husky men's and women's crews.

Crews idle outside Conibear Shellhouse, which was renovated and reopened in 2005 after $18 million and sixteen months of construction, funds that were invested by friends and alumni of UW, including John W. Jacobi.

Annex across the street, and you'll hear a barrage of primal grunts and roars. Strength coaches lead the team through sessions like few found inside a weight room. The accent isn't on raw strength; it's on speed and endurance, just like out on the water.

As Callahan said, "It's a muscle-endurance sport."

Huskies time each rower's reps. They chase each other around stations of the room. They try to get their sets done faster than anyone else. The rowers emerge from this standard workout as soaked as if they'd capsized off their boats into Lake Washington.

Again, EVERYTHING is a competition with Husky crew.

"It's fun," Callahan said of the team's notorious winter workouts. "It's so that you know when you are on that starting line in the race, the one thing you can bank on is that you've competed and you are good at it, and it's not intimidating. These kids really like it. They go home, they compete on grades. They compete on PlayStation."

That's where Callahan's and Ernst's jobs are tougher than many of their college coaching colleagues: in identifying and discovering the intangibles that make a rower succeed.

"In rowing, it's not like soccer where the kid has been competing in it since he was four and you can identify the kid. You are recruiting on physiology," Callahan said. "A lot of kids end up switching sports, say from football to rowing, and they might have a great physiological gift—lung capacity or what have you."

No, it's not like football, basketball, baseball, softball or volleyball, in which recruits are rated and endlessly evaluated with film, coaches' visits and interviews.

"We're looking for personality types," said Callahan. "Are you competitive? Do you have a really strong work ethic? So we identify people early and also pretty late, too. "That becomes a management challenge, to take so many different people from so many different spots. There are a lot of variations and style, but I feel we do a good job of making sure everyone understands how to do it the Washington way."

Conversely, Callahan coaches rowers who come from high-powered, successful national systems, such as Rowing Canada. "These kids know a lot about rowing, and you can't pull the wool over their eyes," he said. "Competition is the best form of development. Our guys are ready to compete during and after going through this program. We teach comparison."

Like Ernst before him, Callahan seeks to get inside a teenager's psyche to find out if he has the makeup to survive Washington's training, let alone compete for the Huskies. Once the rowers are on campus, the focus turns to developing them into international-caliber oarsmen. Washington has a tradition of successful walk-ons, many of whom have won IRA championships, world championships, and Olympic medals.

MANAGING THE BIGGER PICTURE

Oh, but if all Callahan had to do was train, recruit, and develop his rowers...

"Once you become a coach, you realize it's not all the stuff on the water. I mean, the business of running the team financially, to coaching these kids, to making the atmosphere—there's just a lot going on. It's a pretty dynamic position. I think that's what I'm most attracted to...You have to become a fundraiser, a PR-marketing-brand guy, you have to figure out a lot of skill sets."

And you have to have top facilities to create a powerhouse program and attract the international quality featured in the annual Windermere Cup. One of the many beauties of Washington's Conibear Shellhouse, renovated in 2005 from the original, on-campus boathouse built in 1949, is its location: on campus and on the water. "There are other schools that have amazing boathouses, too. Yale built a new one; Cal built a new one; Wisconsin built a new one, (but) I know so many rowers who have to go thirty minutes to a lake or a river," Callahan said.

And it's all-inclusive, with training, locker room, dining, studying and meeting areas in one place for Husky athletes. Instead of commuting to work out off campus, detached from their fellow athletes, Husky rowers are in the epicenter of UW sports. They are housed inside the same building in which all teams eat and study. Washington's compliance and academic-support offices are also inside Conibear, upstairs near the Windermere Dining Room and its sweeping views of Union Bay. "I would say the services we possess here are far and away the best. It's actually given us more exposure," Callahan said. "Our other athletes get to see us coming in

Community support helps make the Windermere Cup the success it is today. Here, spectators and the Husky band enjoy "court-side" views from the banks of Montlake Cut.

from the dock. Hopefully they have some appreciation for what we do. We have appreciation for what they do—our guys are fans of the other teams. So it's made us a central figure on campus, especially the academic campus. I think that's a super-positive thing for us."

The renovation of Conibear galvanized an already-passionate rowing community in Seattle to become even more involved in the Huskies and the Windermere Cup. On any given day at the dock, one is likely to see a Husky recruit, a reporter, alumnus or a local businessman, and even tourists wanting to learn more about rowing or just to see the "boys in the boat" shell from that 1936 gold medal win in Berlin hanging upside down over the dining room.

"It made this a place [where] people are proud to be," Callahan said. "We've gained a lot of momentum with the alumni; we've gotten more connected. It's been pivotal to our success, too. Without them, we wouldn't be doing what we do.

"They've enhanced [the shellhouse] enough where we can regularly compete for championships. There is someone at the shellhouse every day to ride my launch with me and watch practice. We had a coach in this year from Dartmouth. He couldn't believe how many people came by. Even the media attention. We've always had this relationship here, maybe because we started here before professional sports developed. And we've been able to carry it on. Hopefully people consider us a Seattle team, not just a University of Washington team."

That's more of what makes UW rowing—and the Windermere Cup—unique.

For the first thirty Windermere Cups, Callahan, Ernst, Jacobi and Windermere secured teams from China, New Zealand, Egypt, the former Czechoslovakia, Poland, newly independent Lithuania, and other nations across the globe. Their next frontier: a long-standing quest to bring Cuba. That would be a perfect bookend to the first regatta in 1987 when Cuba's former Communist parent, the USSR, raced. "The Windermere Cup has a storied past of looking beyond politics," Windermere president OB Jacobi said, "to bring the best rowers to Seattle." ∎

Barefoot UW crews walk the docks of Conibear Shellhouse, returning from another strenuous sunrise workout on the water.

Photo: Scott Eklund/Red Box Pictures

Windermere Cup Poster Gallery

Since 1988, Windermere has been producing posters for the Windermere Cup using original photography, graphic design, and paintings from northwest artists. Each year's artwork reflects differing perspectives on the regatta. Note that no poster was created for the first year of the event, so Chapter One displays the flyer for the 1987 Windermere Cup.

1988

1989

1990

1991

1992

1993

1994

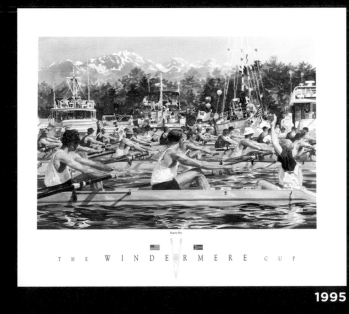

1995

THE WINDERMERE CUP

1996

THE WINDERMERE CUP

est. 1987

1997

The Windermere Cup
1998

1998

THE WINDERMERE CUP

1999

Tradition

The Windermere Cup

2000

2001

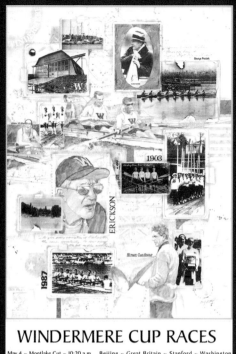

WINDERMERE CUP RACES

May 4 ~ Montlake Cut ~ 10:20 a.m.   Beijing ~ Great Britain ~ Stanford ~ Washington

2002

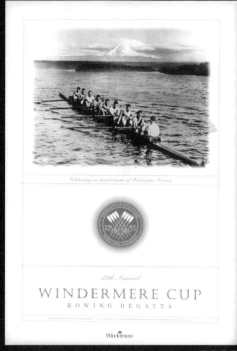

2003

WINDERMERE CUP 2004

UCLA · UW · ITALY · NAVY
Saturday, May 1 · Montlake Cut · 10:20 a.m.
www.windermerecup.com

2004

THE WINDERMERE CUP
established 1987

2005

THE 20TH ANNUAL
WINDERMERE CUP
OPENING DAY OF BOATING SEASON | SATURDAY, MAY 6, 2006 | 10:20 AM

MONTLAKE CUT | SEATTLE
RUSSIAN ROWING FEDERATION
CENTRAL FLORIDA
MICHIGAN · WASHINGTON
WWW.WINDERMERECUP.COM

Windermere

2006

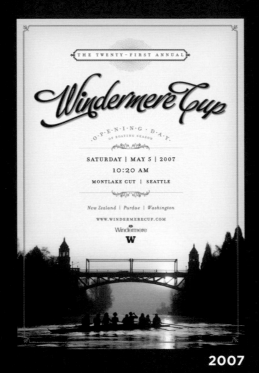

THE TWENTY-FIRST ANNUAL

Windermere Cup

·O·P·E·N·I·N·G· ·D·A·Y·
OF BOATING SEASON

SATURDAY | MAY 5 | 2007
10:20 AM
MONTLAKE CUT | SEATTLE

New Zealand | Purdue | Washington

WWW.WINDERMERECUP.COM

Windermere
W

2007

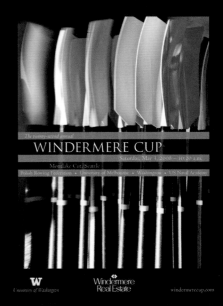

The twenty-second annual
WINDERMERE CUP
Saturday, May 3, 2008 – 10:20 a.m.
Montlake Cut, Seattle
Polish Rowing Federation · University of Melbourne · Washington · US Naval Academy

W   Windermere
University of Washington   Real Estate   windermerecup.com

2008

Twenty-third Annual
WINDERMERECUP

Saturday, May 2, 2009
Opening Day of Boating Season   Montlake Cut, Seattle

Brazilian Rowing Federation · Miami · Oregon State · Washington

2009

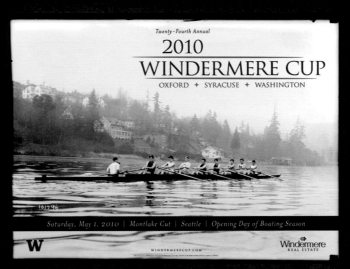

Twenty-Fourth Annual
2010
WINDERMERE CUP
OXFORD + SYRACUSE + WASHINGTON

Saturday, May 1, 2010 | Montlake Cut | Seattle | Opening Day of Boating Season

W   WINDERMERECUP.COM   Windermere
                                      REAL ESTATE

2010

2011

2012

2013

2014

2015

About the Author

GREGG BELL joined *The News Tribune* in Tacoma, Washington, in July 2014 to cover the National Football League's Seattle Seahawks. Before that Bell had been the director of writing for the University of Washington's athletic department for four years. He attended and covered four Windermere Cups, plus the start of coach Michael Callahan's unprecedented five consecutive national men's rowing championships with the Huskies through 2015.

From 2005-10 Bell was the senior national sports writer in Seattle for *The Associated Press*. He's covered multiple Super Bowls, the Olympics, the World Series and Rose Bowls. He also covered the NFL's Oakland Raiders and baseball's Oakland Athletics as a traveling beat writer for the *Sacramento Bee*.

The native of Steubenville, Ohio, is a 1993 graduate of the US Military Academy at West Point, New York, a former Army intelligence officer, and a 2000 graduate of the University of California, Berkeley's Graduate School of Journalism.

He still shakes his head over Callahan, a former Navy brat, razzing him for being an "Army guy" rowing—make that, trying to row—in a Windermere Cup media race.

He and his wife, Wendy, live in the Roosevelt area of Seattle with their twin children, Sarah and Eric.

Bibliography

WORKS CITED

Brown, Daniel James, *The Boys in the Boat*, New York: Penguin Press, 2014

"Cuba without four players for Gold Cup quarterfinal vs. US," *Associated Press*, July 17, 2015

Daves, Jim and Porter, W. Thomas, "*The Glory of Washington: The People and Events that Shaped the Husky Athletic Tradition*," Champaign, Illinois: Sports Publishing LLC, 2000

Kaufman, Michelle, "Cuban defector Osvlado Alonso relishing freedom, MLS success," *Miami Herald*, February 17, 2013

Kellogg, Corey, "Racing Toward Windermere Cup," *The Daily*, University of Washington, April 30, 2004

Malone, Michael, "Hogan's a Hero on Twitter," *Broadcast and Cable* magazine, June 29, 2010

McNerthney, Casey, "May Magic," *Columns* magazine, March 2013

Newnham, Blaine, "Crew Support Draws Top-flight Rowers to Opening Day," *Seattle Times*, May 4, 1995

Peoples, John, "Erickson: 'Mr. Opening Day' – Legendary UW Coach Grabs Microphone, Launches Memories," *Seattle Times*, May 5, 1990

The Reagan Vision for a Nuclear-Free World

Renwick, Danielle and Lee, Brianna, "US-Cuba Relations," Council on Foreign Relations, updated August 4, 2015

"Rewind: Live chat with entrepreneur, humanitarian Bob Walsh," *Seattle Times*, October 23, 2012

Rockne, Dick, "Full Speed Ahead for UW Rowers – Men Defeat Aussies, Aim for National Title," *Seattle Times*, May 4, 1997

Rourke, Mike, "Huskies Perfect in Windermere Cup," *The Daily*, University of Washington, May 5, 1997

Smith, Craig, "Pulling for Lithuania – Rowers from Newly Independent Nation Glad to Shed Soviet Identity," *Seattle Times*, April 30, 1992

——— "Rower Navigates Long Course to UW," *Seattle Times*, May 5, 1995

University of Washington athletic department, "Elite Field Announced for 2001 Windermere Cup," February 23, 2001

University Libraries, University of Washington, Digital Libraries and Special Collections, The Alaska-Yukon-Pacific Exposition

Wogan, Lisa and Morgan, Linda, editors, "Seattle's Most Influential People of 2015," *Seattle* magazine, November 2015

Yanity, Molly, "Windermere Cup: The Perfect Form," *Seattle Post-Intelligencer*, May 4, 2006

ADDITIONAL REFERENCES

Australian government, "Sydney Olympic Games, 2000," last updated November 12, 2013

Bohemia Crystal Glass, Czech Republic

Ernst, Bob, biography and Windermere Cup office files

European Union, "EU member countries"

History of the Seattle Yacht Club

KOMO television's broadcast of USSR vs. US rowing, May 7, 1987

Seattle Mayor Ed Murray, 2014 Windermere Cup/Opening Day welcome letter

Pocock Racing; Matt Lacey

INTERVIEWS

The author also conducted telephone or personal interviews with the following people:

John Boultbee, Daniel James Brown, Michael Callahan, Rob Dauncey, Bob Ernst, Patrick Fitzsimons, Ryan Ganong, Scott Hannah, Jan Harville, Jeanne Hasenmiller, Reiner Hershaw, Jenni Hogan, John Jacobi, John "OB" Jacobi, Todd Kennett, Lois Kipper, Anton C. "Chuck" Kusak III, Seamus Labrum, Mike Lude, C.J. Miller, Sanda (Hangan) Mitchell, Blaine Newnham, Nathaniel Reilly O'Donnell, Sam Ojserkis, Shelley Rossi, Ryan Schroeder, Kestas Sereiva, Michelle Shaw, Robert Squires, Mary Lynn Thompson, Reed Walker (for Sen. Maria Cantwell), Bob Walsh, Jill Jacobi Wood.

Acknowledgments

PHOTOGRAPHY

Red Box Pictures
3131 Western Avenue, Suite 323,
Seattle, WA 98115, USA
(206) 971-7467
www.redboxpictures.com
email: info@redboxpictures.com

Joel W. Rogers Photography
3035 Sheridan Street,
Port Townsend, WA 98368, USA
(206) 849 4186
www.joelrogers.com
email: joel@joelrogers.com

Mike Bay Photography
(360) 710-7129 cell/text
www.mikebay.com
email: mike@mikebay.com

Olivia Bedoyan, Photographer
Seattle, WA
oliviabedoyan@gmail.com

The photographs issued by the University of Washington Libraries, Special Collections Division require written permission from Special Collections. These images may not be sold, redistributed, copied, or distributed as a photograph, electronic file or other media.
Special Collections Division,
University of Washington
Libraries, Campus Box 352900,
Seattle, WA 98195-2900

FROM THE AUTHOR

All the UW and visiting rowers who, since 2005, have wowed me with their dedication, intelligence, and grit.

John Jacobi, Shelley Rossi, OB Jacobi, Jill Jacobi Wood, Geoff Wood, and Windermere Real Estate, for giving me this humbling opportunity to tell the story of their remarkable event.

Coaches Bob Ernst and Michael Callahan, for allowing me inside their rowing dynasty.

Neil Henry and Rob Gunnison, for letting me become a sports writer at UC Berkeley's Graduate School of Journalism.

Maggie Savoy, for rowing on.

Bill Endicott and Tom Negrete, for giving me my start.